Manual for the Soul:

A Beginner's Guide

Manual for the Soul:

A Beginner's Guide.

Awaken to Your Enlightenment in Millennium 2.1

By

Jordan Finneseth

This book was written by Jordan Finneseth based on his studies and experiences. It is the first in a series of manuals that are to the be foundation of Tri-Being: Mind. Body. Energy.

Manual for the Soul: A Beginner's Guide.
Awaken to Your Enlightenment in Millennium 2.1

ISBN 13: 978-0-6927360-3-6
ISBN 10: 0692736034

Library of Congress Control Number: 2016909528

Published June 2016

10 9 8 7 6 5 4 3 2 1

For my mother, Paulette, for her endless love and support, and encouragement.

Acknowledgements xiii

Introduction 1

Section One 5

An Unknown Beginning 5

Chapter 1 7

The Unknown Awakening 7

    Your Unknown Awakening 8

    The Meaning of Life 8

    Sneaky, Lazy, Enlightenment 11

    Memories versus Consciousness 16

    Exercises for Chapter 1 23

Chapter 2 27

The Conscious Awakening 27

    The Breakthrough 28

    Oases of Consciousness 29

    The Human Mind 31

    Do it Consciously-Until You Do it Unconsciously 33

    Progress Not Perfection 35

Chapter 3 .... **43**

Awakenings: Connecting the Dots *43*

Macro vs. Micro 45

Conversations and Perspectives 46

Your Masterpiece 51

Exercises for Chapter 3 53

Section Two **55**

The Stages of Death/Growth *57*

Chapter 4 .... **58**

Denial and Isolation *61*

Denial: It's Not About What You Do, It's About Being

Aware of What You Do. 61

The Choice of Awareness 62

Practical Examples 64

The Need for Proof 66

Isolation 69

Continued Vigilance 71

Exercises for Chapter 4 74

Chapter 5 .... **75**

Anger...*77*

    The Unknown Anger....................................... 77

    Known Anger.. 78

    The Calming of the Seas.................................. 82

    Exercises for Chapter 5.................................... 85

Chapter 6..**89**

Bargaining...*89*

    Bargaining in the Unknown Stage.................. 89

    Bargaining in the Known Stage...................... 90

    Bargaining as a tool for Change..................... 91

    Bargaining to Evolve.. 93

    Exercise for Chapter 6..................................... 98

Chapter 7..**103**

Depression...*103*

    Unknown Anger Turned Inwards: Depression......... 103

    Depression Resulting from the Known Awakening.. 104

    Depression as a Tool For Growth.................. 106

    Exercises for Chapter 7.................................. 109

Chapter 8..**113**

Acceptance *113*

    The Unknown Struggle to Accept 113

    Believing is Seeing 114

    ...Then Comes Knowing 117

    Death/Growth, Acceptance, and Spiritual Lows 118

    Practice Makes Perfect 119

    Exercises for Chapter 8 121

Section 2 Closing **123**

Section Three **131**

    Your Soul's Purpose *131*

Chapter 9 .... **133**

    Mastery through Passion *133*

    The Journey of Life: A Journey of Mastery 133

    It's Not About What You Do, It's About Being Aware
of What You Do 134

    What's My Passion? 135

    You, Yourself and Yours? 139

    Evolution of the Minions 144

    Mastery Through Passion 147

Exercises for Chapter 9 150

Chapter 10 155

Those Who Can't, Teach... 155

Those Who Can, Do; Those Who Can't, Teach......... 155

Teaching, The Inevitability of Mastery 155

Egos and Minions.. 157

Appreciation 159

Teacher Qualification 163

Other People's Enlightenment 167

Exercises for Chapter 10... 170

Chapter 11 175

What Comes After Enlightenment? 175

Life Goes On; The Only Constant is Change 176

Duality and Humanity, Revisited................................ 177

The Return to Stillness, Meditation, and You............ 179

Enlightenment, Magic, and the true Power of Now.. 184

Future Dimensions of Thought.................................... 185

Exercise for Chapter 11 189

Closing 189

Acknowledgements

First and foremost, I want to thank my mother for bringing me into this world and supporting me from the beginning. You are deeply loved and appreciated.

When it comes to the actual writing of this Manual, my first shout out goes to my editor-in-chief and original writing muse Sel. Shades indeed my friend, shades indeed. Cory, John and Joy, your help, support, and numerous long discussions provided me with the material and confidence I needed to complete this Manual, and I am forever grateful.

Reflecting on my own journey thus far and the different spiritual teachers that I have met who have, in turn, attained some level of enlightenment within themselves, I have seen a common thread: the process of trying out different practices and meditations; finding bits and pieces here, and other clues there; and, at some point, "developing their own martial art," and cultivating a unique perspective comprised of inner and outer experience. So, too, is my knowledge and the methods I teach. Much of my philosophy has been influenced by the those of my spiritual teachers, and by no means do I take full credit for its creation. Instead, I have added certain pieces and evolved others to help explain these ancient concepts and ideas to the modern world.

Some of the sages that have inspired me along the way include Wayne Dyer, Alan Watts, Deepak Chopra, Dan Millman, Mike Dooley, S.N. Goenka and the teachings of Vipassana, Yogi Ramacharaka, and Eric Pepin. Thank you all for sharing your knowledge with me as I meander on my mystical path.

Introduction

During the time I was developing the theory for this manual, I read a statistic that stated that Millennials are now the largest demographic that has ever existed in America, defining them as being between the ages of 18 and 34. Being that I am going to be turning 34 in a little over a month, it appears as though I am at the front of this age group, and somehow feel that I am in a leadership role because of that.

From this perspective and looking at the state of the world and the different energies going around in politics, religion, and other world and local affairs, I find myself asking a big question: "What can be done to help change the world?"

Being that we are now the largest demographic in the United States, and understanding that there is energy behind numbers, it is time that we start putting our energy to better use. And in a world full of distractions, consumerism, and screens that change every 5 seconds, it's time to get back to the basics and understand what this game of life is really about. And thus, to clear up confusion and begin moving past the systems of old that have led us to where we are now, it's time to redefine a few things and bring these concepts into the Millennial's 21st Century.

The faiths, dogmas, and traditions of old have led to a current world landscape full of war, opposition to our fellow humans, and a focus on the things that separate us. It's time to release our ego's hold on the past, take an objective view of all the knowledge and teaching out there, and compress it down into its finest, most basic form so that anyone can understand and apply.

In the age of superheroes and Harry Potter, the thing on everyone's minds is bringing magic back into the world. Well, I surmise that the only way to do that is to begin to clear the fog of ignorance and gain a little awareness as to the true nature of reality. With that awareness comes enlightenment, and with that enlightenment comes magic. The way to begin to do this is to stop focusing on the distraction of separation and move forward with our fellow explorers to consciously evolve together.

Who among my generation is ready to "take the reins" of this co-creation we call reality, beginning to shape it into the world that we know it can be, instead of the world that those before us have made it become and continue to do so? A new age of enlightenment has begun, and it starts with a little more awareness.

As a tool to help you through this process, I have developed a workbook that can be used in conjunction with this manual. It is a free gift for people who have purchased this manual as a way to say thank you. It can be accessed on my webpage at tribeingmbe.com/MFTS and the password to enter is **Aware**.

Section One

An Unknown Beginning

Chapter 1

The Unknown Awakening

I remember it as clearly as if it happened yesterday. My mother had just pulled up to the line at a red light and I was sitting in the back seat looking out the window at the street corner. There was nothing specifically interesting or special that I was seeing that led to that moment. It was just an empty street corner with a light pole and a crosswalk button I was passing by on the way to school for the day. But the young child of five or six, who had grown up in a world where TV was just emerging as the de facto babysitter, looked out the window and questioned, "Is there someone watching this – me – like the TV shows I watch?"

Reflecting back now, that was my moment. That was my unknown beginning. I call it the unknown beginning because it is only now, after years of my spiritual quest, that I can appreciate that moment for what it really was. It was my soul, my true being, my future enlightened self, poking through for the first time, hinting at the deeper connection that I would come to understand.

Your Unknown Awakening

The idea that I am proposing here is that there was a time in your past, likely when you were a young child, when you had an awakening. It might not have been some grand spectacle like you see in the movies, where the whole world becomes illuminated and you hear the voice of God. Instead, it was a small, subtle feeling or thought that you had one day. It could have lasted a mere second or stretched for hours, but it was the first time that your consciousness poked through into this physical life and had its first true view of the world.

It was that first awakening that led right to this moment, here and now, as you read these words. Your lifelong quest for answers to unknown questions started at that moment, most of us have just forgotten the significance. And what is most significant about that moment is that it was the precise beginning of your first enlightenment cycle.

Now you may be thinking, "How did this guy go from a random conscious moment on the street corner to enlightenment in a quick step?" And this is where we come to the first big thought introduction and change in perspective needed to get where we want to go. We must start by reflecting within ourselves and removing or changing our definition of enlightenment. Enlightenment is an extremely loaded word, one that conjures thoughts of Buddha levitating through the air or Jesus healing a crowd of people. These thoughts are precisely the things keeping us from appreciating our own evolution.

For the purposes of this book and the treasure hunt I am going to take you on, let's just go with a basic understanding of enlightenment as being made aware of something that was previously hidden or misunderstood by your logical/emotional/reactive human mind. I know it's a simple definition and could just be considered as a part of learning in life, but just work with me here. I am fond of telling people that enlightenment is simple. So simple in fact that it's difficult because us humans like to make things difficult, so for such a big concept to be so simple just does not compute in our minds.

The Meaning of Life

I debated getting into the specifics of enlightenment and the meaning of life until the end of this manual (after you had gotten the full theory), but it seems best to just clear the air from the beginning. Again, don't take it as an end-all-be-all, for it is something that cannot truly be expressed in words, but it's a good place to start.

Working with the basic definition that I have already given for enlightenment, and pooling the knowledge gained from my outward studies of spiritual and religious texts and my inward studies in the halls of my own mind, (get ready for the big reveal...) the meaning of life is to experience it. Every now moment is as unique as the one-of-a-kind snowflake that you are, so combining each moment with your perception of it is what makes your reality. So fully experiencing that reality, wherever you are in your development, is the basic point of our existence.

Sneaky, Lazy, Enlightenment

Maybe this is what the title of this manual should be. It is basically the working premise that helped me arrive at my overall theory, and it clearly requires further explanation.

I like to tell people that I am extremely lazy, and that it's a good thing I have some intelligence, or laziness would be my downfall. When I relate this idea to life and how many of us respond to things when we are given some task that we must complete, even when it is something we enjoy, often times the fact that we have been told to do it really makes us not want to. Like a child who just naturally liked to gather leaves in a pile. Once the parent makes it a chore, the natural interest is gone, and so is the joy.

As a workaround to this tendency, I present the possibility that during the state of the unknown awakening, the things you naturally did as a young spiritual being playing with humanity, as well as the experiences that you had, are all that are needed for you to realize your enlightenment. We just need to remember these things and connect the dots to give you your macro picture of enlightenment.

Without going too far into specifics and citing research articles (Research it yourself and you will have an enlightening journey!), studies have shown that the ability for us to remember what we are exposed to is phenomenal. For instance, if you were to walk past a store window with a display of items, look at it for ten seconds or so, and then proceed on, most people would be able to recall a few general items when asked about it relatively soon after. But if these same people were then put into a state of hypnosis, they would be able to recall every single thing in that window. We are the perfect recording devices; we just need to learn to harness this ability consciously to affect our lives.

How this relates to the topic of enlightenment and your unknown awakening is this: When we are younger, less programmed by the realities of the life we experience, you naturally act more from your "soul." As time goes on, the collective consciousness of humanity sinks in, and we forget these early thoughts and practices, but the lessons remain imprinted on our consciousness. As you progress through the other stages described in this manual, you will revisit these early doings with new eyes, and as the mandala of your mind unfolds, you will see that you have already put in all the work required to be enlightened; all that you need now is a change in perspective.

This is why enlightenment is sneaky and lazy. Spiritual practices, meditation, energy movements...

they are like spiritual homework. And who likes homework? Luckily, there was a younger version of you that just naturally did these things; you just have to find those timesheets and get your back pay. Of course, this is the tricky part. Collecting that back pay does require some effort and homework now, but a new perspective shows it to actually be lifework.

Anyone who has ever given meditation more than just a cursory try may be able to relate to this. You are sitting there, having a really "good meditation" (whatever that means), and some random thought arises of some "bad" thing you did - maybe as far back as when you were a child. First, you may question where that came from, but soon you look closer, realize that you felt guilty for doing that thing, had not yet forgiven yourself for doing it, and then proceed to do so. You realize you were a child learning to play life, and coincidentally enough, after that experience, you never did that "bad" thing again because you didn't enjoy the feeling of the effect it had on others as well as yourself.

From the perspective of this manual, that early experience and the re-examination of it later, learning the truth about life that you learned from it, was a moment of enlightenment. That is a piece of the puzzle or a part of the picture of what your enlightenment looks like.

Remembering Your Unknown Awakening

When I first started explaining this concept to those around me who would become my soundboards and guinea pigs for the theory, one of the first questions I got was, "What if you can't remember this early experience or don't remember having one as a child?" My best and ultimate advice for this is to simply start with the earliest memory of a spiritual/consciousness nature and work from there.

Even if that first moment happened at some point while reading this beginning chapter, that is the perfect place to start. Look how much has changed already. If nothing else, you have this crazy new theory that you have heard and can dismiss shortly, but I'm sure it at least provoked some line of thought different from any you previously had. Close your eyes, go back to that earliest memory, and just feel what it felt like to have that shift.

Next, find some sort of meditation. Now I know I referred to meditation as homework earlier, and to this day it sometimes can still seem so, but it's important. I have my personal preference and will get into that another time, but for the sake of speaking to as wide an audience as possible, just start meditating. Focus on your breath, repeat a mantra, stare at a dot on the wall, listen to a metronome... do something that starts to focus your mind for just a moment on a task that does not require human thought. As soon as a thought arises, which it will, and you are able to catch it, which will take practice, simply return to non-thought.

It is from this non-thought place that the thought of that "bad" thing you did as a child arises. Many are quick to jump on themselves for not having non-thought, but it's all a matter of perspective. Every thought you have is some aspect of yourself vying for your attention. Once it is addressed, that voice will sit back down and rejoin the experience of life.

As you go through this process, practice meditation and begin to learn to quell the shouting voices in your mind as their desires are at least acknowledged and addressed, you will begin to uncover older memories and forgotten truths of youth.

Throughout my known awakening process, I would randomly remember that thought I had as a kid, staring out the car window at the corner. For years the memory would come up, I would quickly reflect on it, and then dismiss it as a normal kid experience. Then I heard it: "True intelligence is the ability to see things from a different perspective."

As I incorporated this "enlightening" knowledge into my being, it began to transform how I looked at things and helped me realize that it was actually something that I had been doing for quite a while. Having studied psychology and worked as a therapist, my job was to try and understand where others were coming from, taking the knowledge that I had acquired about how to help them, and then relating it to them in a way with which their unique perspective would most identify.

The next time my memory arose, instead of again dismissing it as just a random moment from the childhood of a kid who liked to think about television, I instead asked myself why the memory stood out, and I realized that I related to much of the world through television, and thus that was how my higher consciousness best knew to reach out to me. "Is there another audience watching me right now, like I watch television?" And right there embedded in that sentence is a question that any spiritual teacher might use to point out the moment of enlightenment available: Who is this "I" that watches television?

Memories versus Consciousness

The immediate rebuttal that arises in my mind is, "Well, aren't those just memories that you are giving extra importance to?" And, as with all things in this dualistic dimension we find ourselves in, I would say "yes." And "no."

This is not the first memory that I can recall in my life, in fact, it's not even close. At this point, if I really try and am being completely honest, my first real memory is probably from around the age of three, and it has to do with one of those blow-up floating toys that you use in a pool. This toy happened to be shaped like an alligator, and in the scene housed in my memory that alligator was real to that little boy, and he was afraid. Perhaps it was fear itself that caused that memory to be imprinted; emotion has been shown to have a direct impact on our ability to form memories. And there are other memories between that period and the day on the street corner, but that day there was a clear difference.

It wasn't just the conscious memory of life. It was a specific type of inner reflection, a shift, if you will, that rippled throughout time. For me, it was in the back seat of a car, staring at a lamppost, viewing my life like an audience member watches a television show. For my spiritual teacher, it was a day in his youth when he walked into a field, sat on a rock, and looked at the micro life in a pond below him. At the same moment, he saw his reflection as well as the reflection of the sky and clouds above him, with all of the space behind that, and the grander perspective became apparent.

The fact that you are here now, reading this book, I put forward as proof that you, too, have had a moment like this, and it will soon be remembered - if it hasn't already. The theory that I wrote down after my first true meditation and Conscious Awakening was this:

"Your inner-self/guide is you in the future teaching you life lessons ahead of time. All you have to do is pay attention. Or perhaps it is the future self that you want to be, and the psychic part of your mind knows what it would take to get there, and gives you that future self as your guide to self-actualization."

When I read that passage as I was working through the conceptualization of this book in my head, I was astonished. It was as if I could have written it yesterday, but I don't remember it at all. I have come to the realization that like all studious researchers, I developed a theory and then went about putting in the research and legwork (or in this case, mindwork) to prove it. And while the proof in this instance is of a variety that is not easily measured, I leave it to you the readers to put it to the test and report your findings.

Exercises for Chapter 1

1. In some physical form, whether with a writing utensil and paper or on your favorite electronic device, begin to sketch out or form a timeline of your life, and try to remember your earliest moment of 'consciousness.' It can be a little tricky because it may not necessarily be the same as your first memory. I have memories from a very young age, but that day on the street corner was different from all those other memories. See if

you can locate that day. If not, don't fret. Just remember the earliest moment of questioning "what's going on," to put it plainly, and start from there. Even if that is this moment right now, or some moment between starting this book and now, mark it down on your timeline. If you do this and later remember an earlier moment, simply add it in before your previously identified unknown awakening and proceed.

2. Try and remember back to when you were young, and think and feel about what that version of you really wanted in life. If you can remember the first time someone asked you what you would wish for if you had three wishes, think back to the answers you arrived at when you actually gave it thought, later off on your own.

This can be tricky for people with traumatic childhood experiences yet unresolved, so care should be taken and professional help (whatever that may mean to each individual explorer) sought when necessary.

Chapter 2

The Conscious Awakening

It was the summer break between my bachelor's and master's degree programs, and I was relaxing at my mother's house, enjoying the time off from doing anything. I was watching TV (I'm noticing a pattern emerge) when the power suddenly went out. It was late afternoon/early evening, and I found myself with nothing to do because everything that I could think of for entertainment required electricity.

At this point in my life, I had had a few experiences that could be counted as "spiritual" but, again, at the time I had no true understanding of their significance. I had, however, been in the right places at the right times, and had been exposed to the tools that would lead to my deeper understanding. The main such tool, which I learned as part of the Psychology of Stress course, I took during my undergrad studies at Cal Poly, was meditation.

So here I was, sitting alone in the house, the light from the sun waning as the day began to welcome the night, when I heard the word "meditate" come from somewhere inside myself. And as if I had just gotten a suggestion from my oldest and dearest friend, I pulled my legs up under me on the couch, and sitting in a cross-legged position, I closed my eyes and had my Conscious Awakening.

The Breakthrough

At this point in your life, you have spent some undefined amount of time in the unknown awakening phase. We are all on a unique path, so this amount of time will be different for everyone, and no amount of time is any better than any other amount of time. It is what it is, and you are the beautifully unique soul that you are. But regardless of the length of time, your higher self has had enough, has put enough pieces in place, and finally shouts loud enough to break through and have your conscious operating mind acknowledge it. All the hints, clues, spiritual discussions, philosophical insights combined with your life experiences finally produce that first conscious spark of enlightenment.

This is where life gets truly beautiful. The true magnificence is the fact that the number of unique experience of first enlightenment is just as great as the number of beings that there are to have them. You will never be able to find anyone that will have a first moment exactly like your first moment, because it will be completely unique to you and your perception of reality at the moment that it occurs. I think that this is a block for many, because we read about the experiences of others, and then wait and expect to have a similar experience. Instead, we must realize that what others experienced was their own picture of enlightenment, tailor-fit for them, and yours will look much different. This is why I stopped short of telling you my full first experience; that's a description for a different book. This manual is about you.

However it happens – whether sitting in silence during a blackout, basking in the sun atop a mountain, in the middle of a long jog embarked upon supposedly merely to unwind and exercise, or simply looking at yourself in the mirror – the first conscious reflection happens and you are forever changed. Now, from some unknown place inside of you, there is an unanswered question, a twinge that always leaves you feeling – *knowing* – that there is something more, something deeper that you are not seeing.

Oases of Consciousness

This is where the waters of enlightenment start to get murky. Something happened within you, something changed, but much of the landscape seems the same. That profound meditation I experienced during the summer blackout prompted me to conduct some serious research once the power came back on. I dove into all the information I could find about meditation, psychic experiences, and all things paranormal, and combed through the modern spiritual teachers of the time, including Wayne Dyer, Louise Hay, and Deepak Chopra. And while doing that, I also mainly just got back to life and trying to get through it.

The eventual question that arose was, "What exactly *is* enlightenment?" I feel like I had an enlightening experience, but that moment passed and seemingly normal life returned. In my own personal journey, the decade that followed that was full of highs and lows, moments to be proud of and instances of intense shame.

To help form a better working theory, let's refer to these various moments in life, your memories, as dots. My unknown awakening is one dot; my conscious awakening is another. This isn't just limited to these moments of spiritual significance, though. My birth, graduating high school, joining a fraternity in college as well as a relationship that ended with some emotional scars. All these memories, these moments in time are dots. Now you could quickly say like dots connecting your lifeline, but we must look much deeper to see the magic of life.

So it happened, I had that breakthrough meditation, and I dove into research. I had experiences, journaled about them, and as time went on, my focus became more spread out as life does what life does. Amidst all that life, however, moments of focus did return. Even if it was a brief 10-minute meditation or a particularly reflective Aikido practice that focused on the concept of working with chi, moments of your deeper connection, deeper presences are scattered throughout your lived experiences. These moments are your oases of consciousness.

The Human Mind

Our brains are measurement devices. From the moment we are born, we become this catalog of things, ideas, and definitions. This object is that color, that person is this sex, and Adam named all the creatures of the earth. But how do you define the undefinable? These moments of consciousness and breakthroughs to higher realms of thinking make absolutely no sense to the human mind, so it is quick to try and dismiss and forget them. That is the true struggle of awakening. Realizing that the human body and the human mind are not *you*, but rather the tool through which your consciousness experiences this reality.

From a young age, when I thought about topics like witches, wizards, wands, and rituals I found myself looking for the similarities. Likewise, if you view religion with the same lens, you have things like prayer, communion, fasting, and all sorts of rituals. In all these things, there was intent and intender. Now apply the same concept to the human body and consciousness.

Due to their more recent popularity from the *Harry Potter* series, let's borrow the terms 'wands' and 'wizards.' Think of the human body and the human mind as the wand, and your higher self or consciousness as the wizard. The reason different schools of thought use things like rituals, magical objects, and focused intent toward a specific deity or higher being is because the mind needs a workaround so it doesn't get involved. The ritual gives the mind something to do, a task to focus on, which is what the mind does. This allows its focus to be taken up, which allows a higher part of you to 'step forward' and assume more control.

Do it Consciously - Until You Do it Unconsciously

The title of this section is something I tell my students when teaching them how to learn a new behavior. As it came to me as the title of this section, the depth of the statement struck a new chord deep within me. Every act of consciousness - from five seconds of meditation to one good, long, focused "om" chant or simply the contemplation of forgiveness - is an action you take to consciously move your mind aside and allow your higher self to move forward. And just like a snowball rolling down a hillside, before long what might have started as a five-second pebble can become a life-sized boulder.

Each time you venture into non-thought, the unknown, the place where the human mind does not go, it strengthens your connection to that place. (There's that sneaky, lazy enlightenment again!) Throughout history teachers have implored their students to sit and meditate—*just* sit and meditate. Look at your breath, look at water, look at nothing. Just sit still and keep looking. The brain, the human mind, will find all sorts of things. Sounds, smells, sensations, thoughts, feelings, memories, worries, fears, until you find yourself exasperated: "Wait! I'm supposed to be watching my breath!"

Eventually, it gets better. Either that or your mind just runs out of things to define and look at, so it gives up. It 'taps out' if you will. It's not that there is nothing there to see, it's just that the brain doesn't know where to look. It only knows to see what is defined and tagged in its database, and if enough information does not exist, it deletes it from the recognition registry. But that part of you that was finally able to break through and make itself known sees and records everything as well, the only difference is that it can also understand and interpret. You just have to learn that *that* is the real you.

Progress Not Perfection

Duality is just that: dual. Positive *and* negative; up *and* down; in *and* out; male *and* female; good *and* bad.

And, to some extent, so, too, is life and spiritual development. At the time of your conscious awakening, you may ride a spiritual high that lasts anywhere from a few hours to a few days, to even several years. But we do live in a duality; you will also fall back into your old patterns and be challenged to integrate these new thoughts into your being. How else would you really come to understand these truths? "It's easy to be enlightened in a cave," is the quote that comes to mind.

I remember reading books like *The Way of the Peaceful Warrior* and *The Celestine Prophecy*, longing for my own fantastical spiritual tale of awakening. Be careful what you wish for, right? And while it may not be the movie-like story of some 'out there,' as I sit *here* writing this book trying to explain some of what I have learned, I can say that it has indeed been an interesting journey, one full of adventures in duality. And that really is the point to all of this: life and experiences. To have them, be aware of that experience, and to some extent, grow from that experience. Progress, not perfection. A big pitfall to spiritual growth is harsh self-judgement for what one has done or what one thinks that they should be. The fact of the matter is that it is always right now, will always be right now, and you will always be where you are in that now moment that it happens to be. Acceptance of that truth is part of the enlightenment process.

One way to relate it to a simple spiritual teaching is this: even if you were to only spend one second more today in a conscious, aware state than you did at any previous point in your life, it would be progress - and actually a monumental step. That extra second would build into two seconds, then four seconds, and so forth, until one day you spend a whole minute in non-thought, completely forgetting about the now moment when even ten seconds seemed like an insurmountable task. The Enlightenment of Duality is being fully aware of your past and future, while fully living your present, now moment.

Exercises for Chapter 2

1. Going back to the timeline you began in chapter 1, add in the moment in your life when you feel you had your first conscious awakening. The first time that you feel you truly connected with a deeper part of yourself, consciously, and from that moment on you knew you were on a quest for enlightenment, so to speak. Again, even if that moment is *this* moment, or occurred the split second after your unconscious awakening that you decided upon in Chapter 1, bring it into physical form so that you can see it, as well as your consciousness' progression, all while also being able to see such life landmarks as birth and various ages. Again, I stress the

importance of doing this in some physical form, as to bring it out of your non-physical mind and give you a chance to see it from a different *perspective.*

2. See if you can recall the things that you 'wished' for around this time, or the things that you wanted to do or be in life. What were your passions? What was life all about? What do you think brought you to the specific place in life in which you were able to receive that message from your highest self, announcing the beginning to your consciousness' journey?

Chapter 3

Awakenings: Connecting the

Dots

Much like the pictures we were given to complete as a child, the painting of your soul - your enlightenment - first arrives as a sheet with a bunch of dots on it. However, unlike the more simplistic versions we were given as children that also included numbers, this grand "connect the dots" painting that is your life and enlightenment has no numbers or directions to speak of. At least not yet. Hopefully this book can start by providing you with a general map and area to start looking, helping you to learn how to connect the dots and see the picture of your enlightenment.

Probably one of the more difficult pieces of this concept to grasp is to understand that many, if not all of the experiences that will wake you up to the realization that you are enlightened have already happened. The concept of time is what makes this so, but as you loosen the fixed hold that time has on your mind, you will begin to see the beauty of it. Let me take it back to my story to help this make sense.

My first moment of awakening, my Unknown Awakening, happened (as best as I can tell at this moment in time) when that child looked out the car window. What gave me the inspiration for this book was the day, at the age of thirty-three, that I realized that the "person" I thought might be watching my life was actually me, the true me, the highest part of me. I had the information from that experience all along, it just took my mind being in the right state, decades later after years of meditative practice in order to gain some modicum of control over the thoughts that go through this mind.

"When the student is ready, the teacher will appear."

-Buddhist proverb

Some of the oldest sayings hold some of the deepest truths, if only you are able to look from the right *perspective*. And this gets to the main premise of this book: the experiences you have had in your life paired with the intuitive things you have always done hold all the answers and keys that you need to discover your soul and see your enlightenment.

Macro vs. Micro

It is said that true intelligence is the ability to see things from a different perspective. From the time we are born, we see the world from our selfish, self-centered perception. If you think about it, we are just this blank slate with no definitions for anything, and then we begin the process of gathering information from the best level of awareness that we have, and collecting information and perspectives from those around us, who could all be considered our teachers.

We grow, we go to school, we test the knowledge and thoughts that we have, we invest in and expand some things while letting others fall away. For most people, at some point, the journey expands from a selfish one to one of contemplation of our self in relation to others. You begin to learn how your actions affect those around you, thus gaining a new perspective.

A roommate and I once took a trip to Virginia City, Nevada, in search of paranormal experiences. It turned out for that for me one of the most impactful things was as far from paranormal as you can get. In fact, it was the epitome of normal: a conversation that we had with a bartender. The wise bartender revealed the biggest truth that he had come to know at that point on his journey, a point that is embedded in this paragraph itself: life is about conversations. They are our conversations with others that allow us the opportunity to gain a new perspective, completely foreign to what we might normally think or say, adding to our intelligence and overall enlightenment. It's one thing to experience deep philosophical thought or moments of profound insight, but something changes when you share it with another person, say it out loud, and hear yourself say it. This change leads to reflection on whether or not we actually believe that thing. Not only that, but the thought or idea bounces off that other person and they mull it over from their perspective and present it in a new, modified form - a third entity, if you will. Like the process of evolution, giving two people, each with their unique perspective, a single idea to think through, will allow them to combine their collective knowledge to produce a polished/evolved thought distinct from what they might have arrived at separately.

As you go through life, you have many experiences and conversations about those experiences. You grow, you reflect, and you integrate new knowledge gained from these conversations into your being, and the understandings gleaned from such conversations become how you operate in the world. But something else happens alongside this.

While you are growing and evolving as a person, applying your knowledge to the new things that life throws at you, you also have periods in which you reflect back on those past experiences that remain pertinent in your mind. And sure, many of these thoughts will fall to good times and pleasant memories, but far too often it seems that the thoughts that arise relate to a negative experience or something that (to put it generally) does not make us happy.

But why do these thoughts arise and remain, sometimes frequently rehashed in our minds? Perhaps a change in perspective is in order. A good trick that I have learned to help discover the "enlightenment" to be gained from a life experience is to think about it from a micro perspective and a macro perspective.

Speaking from my own experience, a problem with alcohol once led to a series of events that resulted in me being fired from a well-paying job that I had undergone six years of college for. Of course, at the time this loss seemed like a really bad thing, and for years it continued to "haunt" me. But now, years later and the benefit of hindsight allowing me to see the path upon which I was set, I know that what was once seen as purely "bad" actual directly resulted in me sitting in my massage studio typing this book. It was exactly what needed to happen. And not only that, but losing that job was one of the factors that convinced me to stop drinking.

The moment I put all those pieces together, pieces that happened in a micro period, and saw the bigger macro manifestation that is my life, I had a "moment of enlightenment." I understood a piece of my enlightenment puzzle, connected a few of the dots in my overall masterpiece, and saw what that experience/memory/haunting had to show me. And with that new perspective, all the angst that had surrounded that part of my past faded away like smoke in the wind.

Conversations and Perspectives

The reason you are able to experience moments of enlightenment is based on your growth and maturity, both of which I posit come, at least partially, from the conversations you have with others, the differences in perspectives that you are shown, and your ability to integrate those things into your overall being to change how you operate in the world. I had finally had enough internal reflection in conjunction with conversations with others and outward investigation about the reasons behind the incident in which I'd lost my job as a result of my relationship with alcohol, and what the incident had to show me.

And so we continue through life, having conversations and gaining new perspectives. But it is in the moments of stillness, inner reflection, and meditation when the most important conversations take place. They are the conversations with yourself that help you evolve. It is during these inner times that past problems can be given a further review, and with additional perspectives. Perhaps a big life event or influential person came into your life and changed things up, and now you see that past problem as a blessing in disguise. And if upon further review your problem persists, perhaps it simply means that yet another perspective is required, and it can be tabled until another time.

This may give you a new *perspective* on the saying "everything happens for a reason." Let me break it down. The meaning of life is to experience it. If everything happens for a reason, and the meaning of life is to experience, then having experiences and understanding the reason behind them is, indeed, the meaning of life itself. Or enlightenment. Thus, when you have finally gained enough perspective to review something in your life and see what little bit of life magic it had to show you, you have a moment of enlightenment. And, just perhaps, if you can do this for every moment in your life up to this now moment, then you are enlightened.

Your Masterpiece

So hopefully you are now starting to get a working framework. We go through life, generally from our micro perspective, having experiences and doing the general life thing. Some moments are of great importance and highly impactful while many moments are simply normal, daily experiences. All the while though, there is another part of you paying attention and evolving. And it is that part of you that makes those moments important and impactful. It holds onto them, good or bad, conscious or unconscious, because it knows that further examination is required.

This is where you may need to start getting creative and working with your mind. For me, fancying myself a communication specialist, I understand a future version of me is communicating with me through time and space, giving me hints and intuitive leads to help make my journey through life a little easier. If nothing else, that version of me knows how I got there, so it can send past versions of me guideposts to keep me on track.

But whatever form you want to give your inner, highest, *enlightened* self, it is that part of us that beckons us to awaken. It is the part of our mind that remembers the bad breakup or distressing event. It holds on to the memory, longing for the correct perspective to discover the moment of enlightenment that such experiences have to show you. And one day, after one or one thousand hours of meditation, you will take a macro step back and take a look at your life and see something magical. What was once just a bunch of random dots that made absolutely no sense will have all been connected, and a brilliant picture - the true masterpiece that is you and your enlightenment - emerges.

Exercises for Chapter 3

1. This is the point where you can take the timeline that you have sketched or written out and write in NOW. Here we are: the present moment! This is also where the real work of time and patience come in. Start to fill in significant moments, experiences, or realizations that you had that still carry an impact in your life. At some point it may begin to be too much, requiring a piece of paper the size of a wall to sketch out all that you start to remember, but the main point here is to begin to realize these moments for what they were, as well as to begin to look at them from a new *perspective.*

2. In this NOW moment, from a conscious place,
begin to ask yourself, your highest self, what you
wish for, what you want to manifest going
forward from this moment on in your life. If all
the 'needs for survival' were taken care of and
you had an unlimited bank account, what would
you want to create? Where does your passion
lie?

Section Two

The Stages of Death/Growth

In this Section of the book, I reintroduce an old, familiar topic. For many it is referred to as either the stages of death or the stages of grief. However, I think the set of experiences that we will discuss would be better labeled as "the Stages of Growth and Change."

One of the key working premises of this book, which will be further explained in the following chapters, is that it is possible to perceive each moment of evolution, growth, and change as part of this larger process. The severity with which the Stages of Growth and Change impact our life and wellbeing usually depends upon our awareness of the situation and our ability to adapt.

It is important to note that while you will usually find these stages listed in a specific order, the reality is that there is no predetermined progression to the stages themselves. Hopefully after reading this book, it will become clear that in each moment you are simultaneously experiencing all these stages in varying degrees. Since there are so many aspects to our consciousness that are continually growing and changing, some part of you is in one of these stages at all times, and it happens regardless of your level of awareness of the process itself.

This is why life can seem hard. Constant change coupled with our attachment to the past lead to suffering, but ultimately it is experience itself that is the key. Just being aware of these things starts you on the path to finding the peace you seek.

This section doesn't specifically deal with the topic of fear. Long ago, I adopted a working premise that all fear stems from the fear of death. Since this manual takes a spiritual approach to topics usually left to the realm of psychology, many of the "deaths" that occur are really forms of the death of one's ego, which induces the classic model of the stages of grief/death and dying. Some form of change that is occurring within us incites fear from these old ego identities, and we must work through these

stages to accept and integrate our new way of being in

order to evolve.

Chapter 4

Denial and Isolation

Being that time is a choice and that all things must start somewhere, let's start this section off with a couple biggies: denial and isolation. As you will begin to see will be true of all stages, these, too, will evolve alongside you, and many of the things that you thought you'd come to accept and/or laid to rest will have to be revisited and adapted. That is the nature of the Universe, after all.

Continuous growth, exploration, and expansion followed by revision, recycling, and deeper understanding.

Denial: It's Not About What You Do; It's About Being Aware of What You Do.

In its most basic form, denial can simply be seen as *un*awareness, *un*consciousness, or ignorance. In some aspects you may even look at the period of time between your Unknown Awakening and your Known Awakening as a general stage of denial, perhaps one with moments of insight. But that's not to say that denial ends upon your conscious awakening. Even at your most advanced state you will still have old views that veil deeper truths, and those are the veils of denial.

To fit with my longtime tendency of saving the best for last, we're starting with the "less pleasing" aspects of this growth process to get them out of the way and then move on to the "good stuff." And right on cue, this is a good place to address our tendency to define things as either "good" or "bad." The process of expanding your consciousness becomes increasingly more difficult as judgment values are placed on words or concepts. Even to say that you are in denial about something feels like a negative judgment. But that is based on your past definitions of and experiences with the word or concept. For the purposes of this book and this inner journey you are embarking on, let's instead simply look at the concept of denial as a truth or piece of enlightenment that you are still working towards understanding. After all, we are here to learn, grown, and experience, so if we already knew everything and had nothing new to become aware of and discover, life would get pretty boring. So delight in the fact that there will always be parts of this reality that we are in denial about because that simultaneously means that there is always room for more growth and discovery.

To touch briefly on the topic of isolation (which I will go further into later), I will define it as feelings that result from the denial of certain aspects of ourselves. There is a deep part of our consciousness that knows we are cut off from all that we are, and thus some feeling of isolation is the result. The more we grow on this journey of enlightenment and the more we discover more of our true selves, directly correlates to lessening our feelings of isolation.

The Choice of Awareness

For the purposes of this book, let's assume that after the moment of your conscious awakening, each of the moments of consciousness that follow are a choice. You put in time and effort to start exploring and discovering the answers to questions about which you've developed a curiosity. It can be such a simple and subtle change that it can take a while for you to realize you are doing it, but you are actively becoming more conscious, even in little microseconds throughout the day.

This is when the true challenge becomes apparent, and a deeper understanding of the statement "ignorance is bliss" is realized. Awareness is always there, but the amusement park that is the reality in which we live is quite the distractor. Life in unawareness feels like running on autopilot, and it's so easy to just slipstream right into an unconscious, unaware flow of things. Awareness requires effort. Constant effort. This is perhaps the first and most important death/growth cycle to complete and accept, for it will be the launching pad to all future endeavors. From that point forward, it will take continued effort and all of your ingenuity and cunning to traverse the path of enlightenment and uncover the truths about which you may be in denial. For as your mind opens and you become better at weeding out your areas of ignorance, the devices that hold our mind in a lower state get better at veiling these issues from your sight. This is why companions on your journey, those with whom you can openly share and explore your inner dialogues, are crucial in helping gain perspectives about the things to which you may be blind.

Practical Examples

Many early experiences of denial have to do with societal norms and adults misunderstanding children, and these experiences of denial include the period between your Unknown Awakening and your Known Awakening. It is entirely likely that you may have given voice to your earliest contemplations on consciousness, but it takes an equally conscious mind to grasp these deep understandings as put forth in a child's words and then coax them into further exploration.

As you go through this process, reflecting back on the prominent memories of your life, you will surely find moments of enlightenment gold sprinkled throughout your life, as well as subsequent moments of denial. While I was developing the thesis of this book and using my roommates as guinea pigs, one question I got was, "what if your moment of awakening happened in church?" Having my own opinion on organized religions, I quickly remarked, "You're screwed!" It got a good chuckle at the time, but reflecting back on it, that, too, was just another form of ignorance or denial. Having been raised in a Lutheran home and progressing along my own path of discovery, it was inevitable that many of my own early moments of awakening happened through my experiences and teachings in church. Here, too, it comes back to perspective.

One way to look at the denial stage in this process of death/growth could be the denying of questions that come to one's consciousness, but that seemingly go against one's faith. A multitude of possible factors can easily bring about the denial of higher truths, including the fear of losing the community and support network you belong to, or perhaps even the fear that you are losing your mind. As each of these issues arise, they will go through their own mini process of the stages of death/growth, including denial.

To give a simple and clear example, re-evaluating the idea that "There is only one path to God," is a denial process that many seekers from various religions have had to go through. While this is a single example from one faith tradition, opening up to your own unique form of enlightenment will require the surrender and release of many deeply rooted beliefs from the faith in which you were raised. Perhaps this may bring another level of meaning to the saying, "as the student is ready, the teacher shall appear." When you are finally in the right place to release those old fears and move past the denial of what you are experiencing, new understanding will be given.

The Need For Proof

When it comes to matters of the mind and consciousness, one big hurdle and source of denial is the need for actual, physical, scientific proof. One of my favorite jokes is, "We want to be wizards. And to be wizards, we are going to have to travel through the land of madness until we come out on the other side and it all somehow makes sense." The path to the discovery of the soul, enlightenment, or whatever other human word we try to put on this undefinable thing, undoubtedly requires, at least at some point, the use of your imagination. But instead of imagination, as I was taught by my spiritual teacher, change up the perspective and replace it with the word envision. In order to see the micro and the macro (your great oneness with the universe), you will have to envision (use your imagination) what that looks like to you just to give your consciousness a basic construct to work with.

When explaining this concept to people, this is the area that deals with the questions like, "Isn't that just in your head? Aren't you just imagining it?" To this, my short response is usually, "Everything that has ever existed only did so because it was imagined or thought of first." But for the purposes of this section, in a much simpler statement, this question is a clear example of denial. "It can't be that way" or "it can't be that simple, so it isn't so." "It's just in your head." To admit that the truth of reality and consciousness is so simple it instantly makes one reflect upon how difficult we have always made it, and rather than deal with that truth, for most it is just easier to deny it. This simple statement touches on what we will explore throughout the chapters of this section while discussing the stages of death/growth, realizing that denial present is a good step and a clear sign that you are on the path to awakening.

Isolation

Isolation is the inevitable outcome of denial. Once any form of consciousness has been reached, known or unknown, your inner knowledge will be incongruent with any form of denial. What leads to feelings of isolation is the sensation that no one will be able to understand that to which you have awakened. This type of isolation is particularly difficult because it is an internal experience. You can be surrounded by a room full of people who love you, but if you are unable to fully express what you feel and be accepted for it, then you can feel completely isolated. The true lesson and freeing factor is also the most terrifying one: no one else will ever be able to completely understand. Only you will ever be able to understand your unique form of enlightenment because only you know and have been through all of your unique experiences.

You may be asking what the answer to the feeling of isolation is. If you are the only one that can ever truly understand your journey, then by definition wouldn't you always be isolated on your own island of enlightenment?

This is where deeper reflection on the statement above is required. It is the incongruent feeling inside that leads to the feeling of isolation. As if you are isolating a piece of you, from other pieces of you. As you move through the stages of death/growth, with all the micro pieces and micro denials, you reintegrate yourself, thus relieving the isolation. And this is a good place to touch on the concepts of, "As above, so below," "The inner reflects the outer, "Macro-Micro," and so on.

As you progress on this path and go through these inner changes, there will be similar reflections in your outer world. One example, as hinted at earlier, might revolve around a system of belief within which you were brought up. As you awaken to inner truths and begin to integrate them into your being, this will cause friction in your life. Just as an inner piece of you felt isolation as a result of denial, you may go through an outer period of isolation as you become a different person and seek out new individuals that are more aligned with who you are becoming. The more confident you become in your newly acquired knowings, the more you will venture out and make the new you known. Old paradigms and friend groups will fall away, and new ones will take their place. This is evolution. This is growth. This is Enlightenment.

Continued Vigilance

The nature of our reality is such that we must always remain the vigilant student. Our minds and the egos that inhabit them seem to delight in pulling the wool over our eyes by keeping us in denial about certain truths. While our minds and egos only desire to protect us and once served as helpful defense mechanisms, they too must evolve along with our consciousness. To deny this fact is simply that: an act of denial. Which takes us right back to where we started at the beginning of this chapter. Although by definition evolution is an act of growth, so too is it a constant act of death. You are continually dying in order to become the version of yourself that you think you are now, and, in turn, the you that you are now will die to become the you that you think you will become. But you can't die/grieve the you that you thought you were until you get past denying that it is indeed death that is taking place.

Exercises for Chapter 4

1. In terms of your spiritual life, think of any issues or areas of concern that don't match up with your current system of belief and your inner conscious knowing. Any sign of uneasiness or anxiety is a possible sign that you are on the right track. Again, the point of this exercise is not to pass any judgments on yourself or any external system or organization, but merely to bring awareness to the feeling of misalignment. If you would like, from there you can further explore to see if some type of denial exists within you in relation to that truth.

2. In terms of spiritual matters, explore your being and feel for any areas in which you feel a sense

of isolation, in regards to what you may think or believe versus the groups to which you belong and the people you surround yourself with. Again, from a place of non-judgement, just observe and be aware of the feelings of isolation that may exist in you and see what topics arise. If something comes up and you want to put more steps into action, I would encourage you to find someone that might have more knowledge on this topic and can provide a new *perspective*. In fact, find several such people, from various traditions and background, different from your own, and start listening to their *perspective* from a non-judgmental place.

Chapter 5

Anger

Anger. Another one of those words that immediately brings to mind a negative connotation. But when viewed from a different perspective, anger can be seen as one of the most useful tools in our arsenal for survival and evolution. It can aid in helping us overcome difficult obstacles, challenges, or opponents and motivate us to action in the face of adversity as well as be our downfall and karmic professor. And when it comes to this topic of awakening, enlightenment, and the stages of death/growth, the broad topic of anger can likewise be applied.

I feel compelled to take a quick moment as an aside to write a brief disclaimer. Anger is multifaceted and multilayered in all aspects of humanity. I make simple statements here, but there are entire books written on the subject that give it full voice. Instead, approach these words from the perspective of all-knowingness, as well as the spiritual concept of oneness. From a truly philosophical standpoint, even anger directed toward another, from the concept of all-is-one, is anger directed at the self.

The Unknown Anger

As may be intuited from this title, we are starting with the anger that one feels during the time after our unknown awakening. As with the act of awakening to consciousness itself, unknown anger can be experienced at different levels. As you progress along your path, you will come to realize you have numerous conscious awakenings, and with this acknowledgment comes the realization that during the times prior to each moment of enlightenment (even when you thought you were conscious and aware), you were still in a highly unconscious state. And this is where I will do what one of my own good friends on this journey loves to point out that I often do: jump to the end of the discussion. All anger really stems from anger towards the self. Anger about the fact that these simple truths, which are now so clear and apparent to you, have been there all along; it was *you* who could not see them. But this is life, with an infinite number of paths to take and lives to be lived. Soon you will understand that you are exactly where you are supposed to be, always, because that is the unique experience that is your beautiful soul.

Now that I have jumped to the end, let's bring it back to the beginning and work forward from there. In the Unknown Anger phase, anger is directed outwards at the sources in the world that you feel are challenging the beliefs you currently hold. To stay away from extremes, where you start using words like "cults" and "brainwashing," here's a more generic example that may better illustrate my point. Imagine a college student, bright-eyed and bushy-tailed, open to new experiences. Imagine that young soul explorer on a visit home during a break from school, eager to share the excitement of her expanding awareness. Eventually, she brings up the topic of a book of faith outside the tradition in which she was raised, and feelings of concern and anger arise in those close to her. And yet, a similar response might have arisen in that same individual the first time another young explorer of consciousness suggested the same manuscript to them. That was anger.

"How dare someone else suggest to me that they might know something that I don't know, that is better for me?" "How dare they say that what I currently believe is wrong, or at best incomplete?" "How dare they...?"

There are infinite ways that anger can manifest when externalized towards something that challenges our current beliefs. Even after you have had your first conscious awakening, there are many unconscious beliefs and tendencies that are deeply ingrained in your being. In some sense, all anger is Unknown Anger because it is only once the unknown has been brought to light that growth and change can be made. But for the sake of this book and the journey we are on, let's refer to Unknown Anger as the anger that occurs after the Unknown Awakening but before the Known Awakening. Keeping on the same thread as mentioned in Chapter 4, after the Unknown Awakening, incongruence between your inner knowing and outer world will be inevitable. When someone or something comes along and challenges your outer world, many will express anger in response.

I started by saying that all anger was anger towards the self, and from this perspective, the anger that is generated and expressed towards an external source of agitation actually stems from anger about not acknowledging this inner knowing.

Known Anger

Do you know anyone (or are you someone) who is really kind of in-your-face about your need to open your eyes, dispel your false beliefs, and become enlightened? I'm sure I could be seen as this type of person simply by writing this book; I certainly include myself in all these stages and processes. The Known Anger is the anger you feel toward things that you experience as misinformation that distracts others from the truths you now realize. This is especially so for whichever belief system in which you were raised. You have begun to see the truth, and now you are compelled to dispel the lies.

While formulating this topic I was having a conversation with a roommate about my studies into various religions, cults, and groups of a spiritual nature. In many (especially the large ones) you tend to find some really big truths that speak directly to the soul of a person, but there is also a bunch of bullshit that is put in place around such truths as a form of control and manipulation, or, in the very least, ignorance. I won't go into specifics here, but as I gave my roommate examples of this scenario and showed him how the truths that we have been discovering have already been written into different religious texts, but simultaneously masked or misinterpreted, I could see him becoming very angry at the realization that it is still going on. The moment that I saw the anger on his face and felt the energy he was emitting, I exclaimed, "That's it! That's the anger phase of growth!" He had only recently started meditating, and was basically in a spiritual boot camp of sorts through proximity with my cohort, so he was in the Conscious Awakening phase. As the truths he was being exposed to started to change his consciousness, he was also able to see the things holding others in place and veiling these truths from their eyes, and the part of him that once fell victim to that same trickery was not pleased about it. And so, again, we return to the true source of anger.

As was the case with my roommate, anger stems from the understanding that you once believed the same falsehoods that your awakening(s) allow you to acknowledge keep others entrapped, and you are angry about that. Each person is on their own path, learning the things that they need to learn, and experiencing the things that they need to experience in order to bring about their enlightenment. This includes you. And while it is important to keep in mind the unique nature of each individual's journey, trying to help others see the truths that we have come to realize helps to further strengthen our own resolve to continue forging the path of the unknown, traversing the stages of death/growth.

The Calming of the Seas

This is a good place to bring up a topic that you may begin to notice in all facets of this journey. Though it is not always true and can change depending on certain variables, as you progress along your path and become more "enlightened," (I use quotations to emphasize the fact that maybe it's time to think of a new word to address this concept) working through these stages will become easier, and you will begin to integrate new understandings with increased efficiency. The more practiced and aware you become, the more you will begin to see the deeper truth behind a feeling such as anger. It can indeed be a tool, if harnessed in the correct way.

The more you experience the death/growth process, and learn to work through anger, the more it will become a tool for your awakening. It will begin to take less and less time for you to exist in a state of anger and agitation before you become aware of the source of your anger, at which point you can make the necessary adjustments to remedy the situation. Eventually, the mere stirring of the feelings of anger in your body will prompt inner exploration to discover the root and reintegrate the information.

Exercises for Chapter 5

1. Peering through the lens of your spiritual life, look for sources of anger, particularly if that

source is found within your current belief system. Anger is not a bad thing; it is a tool for growth, a trail marker if you will. It helps to point out incongruencies that exist between the way we think things should be and the way that we actually *perceive* them to be. To begin to understand your form of enlightenment, you must start by understanding why the things that make you angry do so, and begin to learn the lessons that anger can teach you.

2. Once you have a list of sources, go over it, from an honest, contemplative state, and ask yourself whether the anger is justifiable in each case, or whether it is an example of the anger of the ego. Are you angry because the source is something you see as a form of control, possibly once controlling you, or is there another source for the anger? Also, take a moment to evaluate if the

anger was useful in some way, or what purpose it served, if any. Again, in the end, it is the awareness of the anger that truly matters. Trust me when I say this: once you become aware of something, your higher consciousness, your enlightened self, is on the task. From that point, it is merely up to us to find the right *perspective* to be able to hear the answer to the question we seek.

Chapter 6

Bargaining

In the general sense, bargaining is the bridge between the old and the new. Your old ego (whom you may recognize as "I," "me," or who you thought you were) is still trying to hold on to its most cherished pieces. In an effort to soften the blow to the ego, you will integrate the information that unfolds as you open up and have new realizations slowly and in stages over time, through a series of concessions.

Bargaining in the Unknown Stage

Much of this section will involve pieces of my own journey as the main bridge to relay information. As with the chapters in this section, bargaining in the unknown stage involves the incongruence between old and new beliefs, and how your enlightened self makes the transition less of a gut-punch to the ego.

My first recollections of bargaining during this phase revolve around my upbringing in the Lutheran church and questions I had about what I perceived as the grander nature of God versus what was written in the Bible. At a young age I quickly saw the mixed message of an all-creating God that would send a part of himself to hell forever as just not making any sense, and from that point on I began to consider all spiritual information (and many truths in general) to be examples of possibilities, but not an absolute. The moment you become an absolute, the opportunity for growth stops.

My first bargain was to hold on to these concepts of heaven and hell, but relate them more to the mental states into which we put ourselves throughout life. Focusing on the pain, sorrow, and negative aspects of life sure seems like "hell" in the present moment, and focusing on the opposite seems like "heaven." I now realize that some piece of me was trying to fit the information that the inner me was shouting into the mold of Christianity; bargaining was taking place to allow certain truths to begin to settle into my consciousness.

Bargaining in the Known Stage

In the known stage, the bargaining that you do becomes much more apparent. As the old "you" slowly starts to fade away and the future "you" begins to emerge, much of what your life looks like will change along with it. The people you know and spend time with, the places you go, the activities you do with your time, and the information you pursue will all begin to shift and change.

A bargain that some people make as they explore the known stage is to continue to attend events of the church or faith in which they were raised, not because they fully believe or subscribe to that doctrine, but rather to appease those close to them, either out of love or a desire to avoid making waves. For those not raised in a religious household, similar bargains may be made. They may find themselves participating in activities they once enjoyed, but will notice something has shifted; while they still value spending time with those they love, they will start to experience the feelings of isolation described earlier in this chapter. As you move more and more into who you will become, these old bargaining chips will begin to fall away; you will no longer require a placeholder, and the spaces revealed without them will be filled with new pieces that are more aligned with your inner knowing.

Bargaining as a Tool for Change

The experience of moving beyond bargaining can also come in the form of releasing old, non-serving habits to allow for new, self-evolving ones. A particular struggle in my life that was a big piece of my journey revolved around alcohol. Despite all the good things I did in my normal life and the progress I made on an inner level, I refused to release my attachment and physical enjoyment of alcohol, despite all the harm it caused in my life and the lives of others. Even worse, in my case, alcohol enhanced certain aspects of my spirituality, including my ability to tune in to people, while inhibiting the inner filters that know how to either relay that information in a tactful way or abstain completely from doing so when the information is not useful. But even that experience was part of the lesson tailor-fit for my growth.

At that time in my life, the experiences I had while intoxicated usually led to negative outcomes, but because the normal governors that dictate my behavior were not in place, I was also able to see the deeper connection that exists between everything (and I mean everything - you, me, your computer, the planet, the sun... The Universe) and the things we are capable of. Many of those negative experiences are what led me along the path that resulted in me being here, writing this book, so in the grand scheme of things, they were exactly what needed to happen. There is a well-known story, often attributed to Buddha, that will help explain the premise of this concept, and perhaps help you to see how to connect the different parts that will aid you in beginning to see your enlightenment picture.

There is a farmer in a village. One day, his fence falls down and his stud horse runs off. Immediately all the other villagers come up to the man and start saying how bad and unfortunate this is, and how he won't be able to do his farming without his horse. The farmer simply states, "Good or bad, who knows? We'll see."

Out of nowhere, a day or two later the horse reappears, running right back into his enclosure, accompanied by four wild mares that he found in the wilderness. The farmer simply walks over and puts the fence back up, and now he has five horses. All the villagers come up to him and begin telling him how lucky and fortunate he is, having increased his wealth immensely. The farmer simply states, "Good or bad, who knows? We'll see."

A few days later the farmer and his son are out working with the mares, trying to break and tame them. One of them is particularly difficult and ends up throwing the farmer's son off, and he subsequently breaks his leg. All the villagers come up to him and begin saying how bad this is because he needs his son to help him with the work around the farm, and how will he get it all done now without help. The farmer simply states, "Good or bad, who knows? We'll see."

The following week, the local warlord came marching through town and they collect every able-bodied young man to go off and fight in a war. Eventually, it winds up being a failed campaign, and everyone that went was killed; the farmer's son was spared this fate since his broken leg made him incapable of walking. "Good or bad, who knows? We'll see."

Many people looked at me with sorrow for the struggles that I went through with alcohol, but I was going through my own death/growth cycle. Looking at my life now from a macro perspective, I can see the trail of events that led me to this moment. I was fired from a good job, prevented from getting similar and even "better" jobs, and I spent a period of time unemployed. But I also went back to school and studied massage and environmental health, and most importantly, I had the free time to dedicate towards my self-development. Instead of helping others, I was forced to help myself. "Good or bad, who knows? We'll see."

Let's tie these examples in with the experience of bargaining. My growth process with alcohol started as a young man completely rejecting the prospect of never again drinking a drop of alcohol in his life. That option was too daunting; alcohol was simply too enjoyable, and complete abstinence didn't seem worth it. However, after experiencing a few consequences, the bargaining floor opened, and several options commenced: only certain types of alcohol, only on certain days, only with friends, etc. Bargains were reached, compromises were made, but the consequences continued to get worse until the stage of acceptance was reached. And even at that point, the struggle continued. But it was far easier, and it continued to be so until this new aspect of myself, capable of seeing life without alcohol as a vast improvement, had been fully integrated into my being. A clear piece of my enlightenment picture was made visible to me.

Bargaining to Evolve

Bargaining can be harnessed as a tool for your evolution. Thinking of big, life-altering changes or monks levitating in a cave can be an extremely daunting prospect, so little steps and bargaining can help to ease the transition. At one point, I was unable to say with certainty that I wouldn't drink for a year, but I completely knew that it was possible not to drink for an hour or a day. Opening bid: Never drink again. Return offer: Don't drink for the next day. It may not have been much, but bargaining had begun and a change was made.

I use this example in my own life just to illustrate a point. If this or a similar topic happens to be a struggle in your life, and in keeping with the message of this book, please don't measure your ability to deal with it as compared to mine. It takes us how long it takes us, our journey is completely unique unto us, and we all have our own life path and picture of enlightenment.

For the purposes of learning how to use bargaining as a tool, it might help to look at it as an act of coming into balance. After all, we are spiritual beings having a human experience. Your enlightened, highest self, soul, or whatever term you prefer to try and describe this experience that is not of the physical, earthly realm, is only one side of balance. We may have some grand idea or definition of enlightenment, but the fact remains that the point of life is to experience it in human form. Enlightenment can be seen as an ever-evolving and changing perspective, but that perspective is cultivated through the sensory experiences of a *physical* being. Bargaining can thus be seen as the place where spiritual meets physical, and the metaphorical deal for the current life experience is struck. From that point on, some days will be spent more in the spiritual realm, some more in the physical realm, and some balanced in between. What matters most is the awareness of the experience.

Exercise for Chapter 6

1. Think about your current system of belief and consider which bargains you may be making involving what you feel on the inside and what this outside structure requires of you. For example, perhaps your school of thought says you must use a specific talisman in order to channel higher knowledge or healing energy, but you feel it is not needed; perhaps you consider yourself to be the talisman and pretend

to use the physical object for appearance sake. If you have already been aware that you were doing this, great! If not, congratulations-you are now! Remember: awareness of the choices you are making is all that is needed.

2. Pay more attention to the bargains you make when it comes to the people you talk with and share your innermost thoughts. If you have a close group of friends with whom you find yourself translating your own 'spiritual lingo' into the words of their creed or faith, simply be aware that this is a bargain you are making with yourself as you slowly step towards your own enlightenment path and away from that of another. Remember: we are all on our own unique path that no one else can walk for us.

Chapter 7

Depression

This may be one of the most impactful areas of this book on your journey, so I feel it is worth slowing down to highlight that significance. While this book will use the lens of spiritual growth to view the subject of depression, I also come from a background of clinical psychology and understand that each person's journey with depression is unique. While it is my hope that this book will help guide you, move with compassion, and know that your journey may be complemented by personalized professional assistance.

Unknown Anger Turned Inwards: Depression

As I sat thinking about how to begin this chapter, the first thought that came to mind was a quote I learned in school about depression: "Depression is anger turned inwards." That seems like as good a place to start as any!

By now you've probably grasped the flow and general philosophy of this book, and it will come as no surprise that here, too, we can use the macro-micro perspective of awakening to start connecting the pieces that form your larger puzzle. During the unknown consciousness phase, the inner you (your highest self that poked through in that first moment of consciousness) is yearning to be acknowledged. As it starts gaining strength and "punching through" more and more as you approach the moment of your conscious awakening, it can often manifest as depression.

If from a psychological standpoint depression can be seen as anger turned inwards, then the depression that we experience on our spiritual journey may actually be the result of anger our inner self feels towards the incongruence it sees between what it knows about the world and the lack of acknowledgement of those truths by you, the operating consciousness. Many gentle, spiritual people abhor the idea of hurting others or directing anger at them, but the energy has to go somewhere, so instead it gets turned inwards and manifests as depression.

During this unknown phase, anger could also arise from external triggers, such as another person challenging your beliefs. What I propose is that the anger stems from an inner knowing that *agrees with* what the person presenting the challenge is saying, but the knowledge cannot be integrated into the conscious operating self until this growth/death process is complete, leaving the inner you yearning to acknowledge its deeper understanding and newfound truths.

Depression Resulting From the Known Awakening

After the moment of your conscious awakening, sources of depression of the unknown variety can still arise. Some the strongest causes include desire, expectations, and putting others on a pedestal. The latter of these tends to happen when you start to compare where you are on your spiritual progression to where you think you should be, but especially when you compare your journey to that of others. This is not a new topic, but rather one of the oldest, which should be re-approached with new eyes. Think about it: in most parts of the world (and likely your whole life) you had a Jesus, Buddha, Mohammed, etc., figure to whom you were to hold as your spiritual role model, upon whose life you were expected to emulate your own. Perhaps you've spent your whole life unable to follow in one or all of their footsteps. Of course, such an impossible standard of expectation can lead to feelings of depression; this is especially so once the inner you starts to shout out, letting you know that you have always been (and will always be) as perfect as they were, just as you are now.

I've heard many people say that they were not pleased with themselves because they felt that they hadn't meditated enough because so-and-so meditated longer or did so much more. Judging yourself based on the actions and life of another, and deeming yourself inferior and thus less worthy by comparison, is a common spiritual source of depression that can cause us to become stagnant on our path and stop progressing. I promise that if you were to spend twenty-four hours a day for a month with the person to whom you compare yourself, you would not put them on the same pedestal. And the same goes for every other person you have ever met or thought about or will ever meet or hear of - be they a famous movie star, an athlete, the Pope, or the Dalai Lama. We are *all* having a human experience, which means that we *all* have some things with which we struggle. Learn to take everyone off the pedestals upon which you have placed them, and inversely, remove all feelings or notions of being superior anyone else, and you will see your depression melt away like ice on a hot summer day. Every one of us is on our own unique path, exactly where we are supposed to be at every moment in time because that is where we will find our next puzzle piece or dot along our unique path to enlightenment.

Depression As a Tool for Growth

As with every chapter in this section, we explore ways of integrating the knowledge and awareness of this topic into your tool belt for growth. First and foremost, the feeling and experience of depression must be fully acknowledged, felt, and observed for a period in order to be addressed. We are here to experience all of what it means to be human, and that includes being depressed.

Here's another way to look at it. Behind every experience of depression there is some source. For the purposes of this book, we are identifying that source as your inner enlightened self yearning to break free. If we try to ignore, hide from, cover up with medication, or simply mask the depression, we are missing a valuable trail, a treasure map if you will, back to a bit of your soul, your enlightenment. If, instead, you moved into the depression, fully felt it, embraced it, and experienced it for each of the 'now' moments in which it exists, you would be able to examine it much more deeply and get back to the source. And when you do that, you will see the deeper lesson and the piece of your soul puzzle that is a moment of enlightenment. And you will have connected another dot and brought your enlightenment picture that much more into focus.

Exercises for Chapter 7

1. Look for sources of depression that arise from a feeling of not living up to the expectations set by your current spiritual/belief system. Maybe life has been really busy and stressful lately, and you haven't found time to meditate three times daily like your guru demands. We can easily fall into the, "I must not really be dedicated or truly spiritual because I am unable to balance life and fit in what I've been told it takes to be

enlightened." What you may now be beginning to see is that what others suggest may simply be what *their* enlightenment process requires of *them*. Remember that you don't have to make any changes with this exercise; just be aware of potential sources of depression, and your higher self will begin to get to the source.

2. Find someone you can talk to, a confidant to whom you can safely express this incongruence aloud. If you are unable to do so with a friend, family member, or spiritual leader, consider going to someone or somewhere where no one knows you in order to find a person to whom you can express your doubts. If you are a Catholic, say it to a rabbi whom you may never see again. Heck! You could even call a psychic consultant and pay for a few minutes of time to express your concerns. This exercise allows us to

take further action and another step on the path

to simple awareness: venturing into the land of

exploring new *perspectives*. Go at your own

pace. Awareness is the key.

Chapter 8

Acceptance

Acceptance is when all the pain and suffering that we have put ourselves through finally pays off, or we have studied a new piece of information closely enough, deemed it worthy, and begun the process of integrating it into our being.

The Unknown Struggle to Accept

It's no coincidence that on the day I was thinking about writing this section I had a discussion with a client that revealed a very good and relatable example of how the stage of acceptance functions in the process of awakening. My client, a mother whose children are now adults, shared with me that she has been experiencing anger her eldest son expressing towards her. She was able to pinpoint the start of his anger as having begun all the way back to when the man who he has become was only a young boy of seven. Since that time, this problem has always been present, manifesting in various ways through their interactions. Finally, the week before I wrote this chapter, she came to a moment of acceptance. This mother began to accept the fact that her son's anger towards her is now and has been since its inception, *his* problem. She realized that there is nothing she can do or say to change his perspective; the lesson is his to learn, and it will be his enlightenment journey that will be impacted by the what occurs along his path. Her piece was to learn, as a parent, to realize that her child is his own person who will have to go through his own growth cycle. She described the moment she realized these truths as a weight having been lifted off her shoulders, and a new level of awareness flooded in.

When you look at this situation from the perspective presented in this book, hers was a moment of enlightenment that was about thirty-five years in the making. It took all that time for her to go through the stages of death/growth in order for that moment of insight to afford her an enlightening perspective. She realized that she is on her own path and that her son is on his own path; the only path that we can ever really do anything about is our own. On a conscious level, my client had known this for a long time, and even taught it in her own healing practice. But to really experience it and understand it in her own life took time, and ultimately acceptance.

Now you may be thinking, if she had this realization while doing a spiritual coaching call with me, isn't she in the known phase, not the unknown phase? I completely concur. Even know I flash back through the titles of this section, searching for the flaw in my theory. The only conclusion I arrive at is that for the purposes of this book, the starting point of my theory begins at your unknown awakening, and inextricably tied to that moment of awakening has always been the *acceptance* of that awakening. Thus, despite all the stages of death/growth, acceptance was the initial requirement. Acceptance is the first stage of awareness, of consciousness, of Being.

Believing is Seeing

Approaching spiritual matters from a scientific standpoint is difficult because science needs proof. In other words, for science, seeing is believing. But when it comes to matters of the spirit and the places you seek to go with your mind, going out on a limb and believing before seeing is the equation that is required.

To give a very common, relatable example, let's talk about money and the power of manifestation. Every teacher has their definition of manifestation and way to go about it, including me. Regardless of the ritual or train of thought you choose to make it work, in the end, consciousness begins with the acceptance of the law of manifestation. At its most basic nature, everything is made of energy, and in this dimension that elemental energy manifests into what we know as the "physical form." How that process takes place and who or what is doing the manifesting is where it begins to get more complicated, but the initial acceptance that the process is occurring remains paramount.

...Then Comes Knowing

After you have dedicated some time to your path, pushing the limits of sanity and normality, asking internal questions that you dare not say aloud for fear of committal to an insane asylum, you will arrive at a place of undeniable knowing. You may have long ago accepted the fact that you would have to believe things that you cannot see in order to get where you want to go. If so, your diligence and dedication are about to pay off in a big way.

It is the path of the sage, the seeker of truth that propels us to this eventual place of acceptance and seeing the bigger picture: it is one thing to believe something, it is another to know it. Even the scientific stance that "seeing is believing" can be critiqued as fallible. To use a more physical/literal understanding of the phrase, one could say, "yeah, but your eyes can lie to you." The common saying about belief lies right in the middle of the word: beLIEf. Your beliefs will lie to you. When you truly and fully explore and experience these cycles of growth/death, you will leave the experience of believing behind, instead arriving at a place of profound *knowing*, with those truths being written on the fabric of your soul.

Death/Growth, Acceptance, and Spiritual Lows

Looking back on my own spiritual journey, there are marked periods of seemingly low spiritual activity or advancement, where my meditations fell off and I just really wasn't feeling it. Clearly at some point these periods ended, or you wouldn't have this manual to read right now. And while there can and are many explanations for these valley-like periods in our spiritual development, at a most basic level it returns to the acceptance of new truths and the dying away of old ones.

Newer beliefs, and those less firmly held, fall to the wayside like rain in a thunderstorm, but old beliefs that have been part of us for as long as we can remember will not go so quietly down the storm gutter. Thus, we go through the stages described in this section until we finally arrive at acceptance. And acceptance isn't pushy; it will give you all the time you need.

This reminds me of another favorite saying of mine. (How many favorite sayings do I have, anyway?) The infinitely patient man has everything he ever desires. Regardless of where you are and where you think you should be, you is where you is. Accept that fact. And at the same time, become aware of and accept another universal fact: the only constant is change. You are always exactly where you need to be, and soon, you will be somewhere different. All that is needed for that change to occur is patience.

Practice Makes Perfect

As I find myself searching for where to go next on the topic of acceptance, the phrases 'practice makes perfect' and 'fake it till you make it' come to mind. Learning to more easily accept things takes practice, and even if you don't fully accept or understand what is going on with you right now, put on a poker face and tell yourself that you accept it anyway. One way or another, you are going to go through the stage of acceptance; you might as well do so as consciously as you can while you are capable of awareness. Simply thinking about acceptance - even with something that you flat out, completely do *not* accept it - at least allows room for a new perspective to emerge, and the act of creation has begun.

If you look back on your life to when you were a child who threw temper tantrums when you didn't get your way, you will clearly see progress on your path of acceptance. When you find yourself not knowing where to go or feel stuck in a rut, reflect back on where you've been and how far you've come; you may just realize that you were merely taking a well-deserved vacation in this game of life. If change and acceptance were easy, we would all be enlightened and there would be no need for this manual. Of course, I dare say that this is not the case, and I am pretty sure that it is possible to miss the challenge of growth and change and the magic that is our unfolding path of enlightenment. So accept where you are and delight in where you will go, for that is the magic of the ever changing *now* moment.

Exercises for Chapter 8

1. This first exercise is going to be a little different than the ones you have done previously. Instead of thinking about a current situation, I want you to reflect back and think of a time in your life when you had a spiritual breakthrough that led to a transition from an old way of thought into a new one. This will be a moment in your life when some long held, egocentric beliefs from a perspective that no longer suited you finally released its grip on your consciousness, and you had a moment of enlightenment or understanding. Once you've identified such a memory, examine it closer for the acceptance that took place in you. Recall the feeling from the exact moment in which you released that last bit of grip on the old you, and moved into a

new way of being. Tag and remember that feeling, for it will be the feeling that will set you free.

2. Think about a current situation in your spiritual life, a part of your spiritual progression that you feel you are on the brink of having a breakthrough. You feel the release of an old pattern coming on, but there still remain a few more resolutions that need to be reached internally. If you can find this area within you, I want you just to reside there for a brief period, however long feels necessary for you. Next, recall the memory, moment, and/or feeling you explored in the first exercise. Recall that feeling of acceptance, and then layer it upon the current situation that has come to your awareness. Experience what the acceptance of this new truth feels like to your Being. As with many of

the exercises in this book, the most thing is to

simply be aware; in this case, your awareness

will be of the fact that you are going through the

acceptance process.

MANUAL FOR THE SOUL:
A BEGINNER'S GUIDE

Section 2 Closing

In closing this section, I want to return to something previously stated. As you are beginning to see, much of our defined reality is really a matter of perspective. As such, it is important to reiterate the perspective of this manual, which is that we are spiritual beings having a human experience.

Every aspect of this guide, from the title to the language used in approaching each topic, comes from a spiritual view of the world. That being said, I also hold the perspective that the common psychological concept of the stages of grief (and death and dying) can potentially be applied to every change that one goes through in life. If you prefer to remove the spiritual perspective but still find meaning in the basic premise, you will nevertheless be a changed person. The only inevitability in this life is change, and the suffering we experience is usually the result of some form of ego attachment to a no longer existing past. Learning to embrace change and adopt new perspectives as a general mode of operation will help to make life run more smoothly.

If any of the areas discussed in Section 2 have brought about thoughts, feelings, or memories that feel as though they are too much to handle on your own at this moment on your journey, remember to seek out a new perspective, preferably in the form of a professional's help (whatever your definition of a professional may be).

Section Three

Your Soul's Purpose

Chapter 9

Mastery Through Passion

We pick one thing and learn to master it, but why do we really do this? Most of us in society today view things through the lenses of work and money. I learn these skills and master this profession so that I can earn enough money to live the life I deem comfortable. We may pick up hobbies that keep us active and engaged, but what else do you use your free time for? While we could delve into a deep philosophical discussion about the nature of time (and how it doesn't really exist), the fact is that in this physical life, in this physical reality, the time we have here is not certain. Even the healthiest individual that eats all the "right" foods can fall victim to the random accidents that take people's lives every day.

The Journey of Life: A Journey of Mastery

By now you have the basic framework of how to work on your "soul" and find your unique form of enlightenment. Does this mean that the goal of life has been met? What is all the rest of it about? These are the questions you find yourself asking once a certain level of understanding has been attained.

Here is where we overlay this concept with actual, real, everyday life. It is also where I address the idea of enlightenment as the journey, not the destination. Becoming "enlightened" to the beauty of your unique life, your journey, is something that only you can do. Even in that *now* moment at which you feel you reach some form of "enlightenment," it will still be a *moment*. There will still be more life afterward, and changes will still occur.

So where do we go with all this? You've developed a deeper appreciation for different moments in your life and have grown in your perception of the world. Now it's time to turn that awareness, that focus, towards what you are passionate about. And to do that, you can again look to the things that you have always done.

It's Not About What You Do; It's About Being Aware of What You Do

Throughout your journey in life up to now there have been various things that you have done. Some of them you did because you were told to; some you did because you were vaguely interested, and so you dabbled, and other things completely engulfed your curiosity. But behind even all of that, there is something else you are doing. Something that is your specialty. Something significant and so much a part of you, that you most likely don't even know you are doing it. It is how you get things done.

This may be a difficult thing to identify because this thing is basically your modus operandi for your intuition and highest self. For me, I look at something, analyze it from multiple perspectives until I reach a deeper understanding, and then feel an insatiable urge to share that understanding with others. For a friend of mine, he recently realized that, conscious of it or not, he tends to say or do the thing that brings about change in an environment. Let me give an example.

My friend is a young man who works with the aging and elderly. He began observing all the goings-on in the organization for which he works, seeing clear flaws. He noticed colleagues who were set in their ways; conflicts amongst and between different staff groups and levels of management; and superfluous bureaucracy. Even though he is pretty close to the bottom rung in the hierarchy, when he chose simply to voice some of these observations in a staff meeting, he sparked changes that could be seen throughout the organization. It was reflecting upon this and similar events that took place during our brief friendship/mentorship that allowed him to realize that he is an agent of change.

My friend's intuition led him to speak up in situations in which he can start rolling the snowball of change down the hill to get things going. And, if you think about it, that's what most of us (and the world at large) need right now. This young man simply set out to care for others, especially those who are experiencing the transition that is the end of life, but in so doing he was really learning to cultivate his art - his enlightenment - as an instrument of change.

It's not about what you do; it's about being aware of what you do. Once he was aware of his role as an agent of change, he gained a new perspective about it, becoming a little more "enlightened" and able to see his overall masterpiece. Now he is able to harness that ability from a more conscious place in order to effect greater change in the world moving forward. This all came about by reflecting on past events from a new perspective that allowed him to see what he was doing that was unique to him.

And so we return to the premise of this book: you've already had all the experiences you need to understand your enlightenment; all that is needed is a new perspective. This reminds me of a quote I recently heard, and as I think on it, I gain a new perspective, or a little bit more of my *own* enlightenment: "As soon as a problem is created, so is its solution. All that is required is the right perspective to see it." By this point we can consider this quote as it relates to this manual: If we believe ourselves to be unaware/unconscious/unenlightened right Now, our enlightenment already exists; it's just a matter of finding the right perspective in order to see it.

What's My Passion?

It's important to address (or re-address?) something at this point. Although this manual has been laid out in sections and in numerical order and such, know that many of the processes that are being discussed are happening at the same time. Whether in your conscious, unconscious, or "more enlightened" state, new lessons in life continue to be learned. Things happen that continue to push you out of your comfort zone; you simultaneously experience various stages of the death/growth cycle pertaining to a variety of inner issues; and, oh yeah, there's the whole bit about life and duality. That is why different practices that help you understand macro and micro perspectives are crucial in helping you continue to develop.

Let's go back to that bit I just mentioned about life and tie it in with your "passion." Looking back now, having started to see some dots and make their connections in your overall masterpiece, you may notice that many of those significant moments were, again, the things you just did naturally. The way you made things uniquely your own.

When you were younger, and your life was more controlled by those older than you. Yet, even with the things that you were told you had to do, you were able to find a way to make tasks at least a little more enjoyable or bearable. As you got older, things like school, work, relationships, and a host of other responsibilities come up in life, and these become the "things we are told we have to do." Throughout all of that, we find some way to make those things at least a little more enjoyable or bearable, and that thing we choose to achieve *that* goal is our passion.

In my case, I say that I am a healer. No matter the situation I am in, at some point if I can help heal myself or someone else, or, taking a more macro perspective, give myself or someone else a new perspective with which to look at an experience or situation to gain another moment of enlightenment, then I am contented. Early on this manifested in the form of finishing my schoolwork, then turning to my classmates to help them understand how to do the assignment using their own strategies. During college, I started off in aerospace engineering, and eventually graduated with a bachelor's degree in psychology before going on to get a master's and work as a therapist for a little while. I helped give people a new perspective on their own minds. After that I studied massage therapy and other forms of healing the physical body, and even when times were tough and money was tight, what really mattered to me was when I helped give people a new perspective on their bodies and how they can feel better, healthier, and generally less affected by the physical toll of life. My passion, after reflecting on all those little enlightenment dots, was teaching.

This is a good moment to see a little of this process in action and also show you how a lot of the process is happening at once. If you've already begun looking back at the memories of your life that stand out to examine them and test out whatever this concept I'm talking about regarding "discovering your insight of enlightenment from every now moment of your life", you can add the perspective that your insight might also be something that hints at your passion. And when you see that your passion is intertwined in that moment, you may just experience one of those fabled "flashes of enlightenment."

And this is where we can finally talk about one of those big topics: faith. But, as you might have guessed, it's time to throw out old notions and redefine faith in a new light. Regardless of what it may be, for the purposes of this book, that which we usually refer to as faith in life, will simply be referred to now as trusting and being willing to try something out in order to see if there's anything there to be learned, gained, or understood. For example, I am asking you to have faith in me and my proposition that if you look at these past moments long enough, you will begin to see your passion. If you want to, you can use me as your placeholder, thus freeing you for further exploration. You may tell your higher self, "he said it's there, so this isn't just coming from me, and I'm not to blame for this wasted time." But really you are merely using yourself as a placeholder so that you can truly explore more deeply.

You, Yourself and Yours?

There sure were a lot of "you's" in that last sentence. What's that all about? And just what does it have to do with mastery and passion?

Eventually, you will work out your unique way of understanding this topic, but let me give you a basic starting point to help get it going. Aside from the deeper spiritual concept of the Three Selves, embodied by the trios found in many religions (such as the Father, the Son, and the Holy Spirit in Christianity), and a topic that will require an entire book to even begin to explain with the depth it merits, you have many "I's"/ "me's," "voices," "personalities" or for lack of a general word, "focused versions of yourself with a specific 'want.'"

The best word that comes to mind brought a smile to my face when thinking about the movie series that popularized these loveable little characters. I will refer to the "I's" in our mind as minions. The problem with the unconscious is that the minions are running the show, and they've managed to convince you that they *are* you. Following the same thread, let's consider the following example.

It's Friday night, you're bored, and there's nothing on TV, so you decide to go to the movies. When you arrive at the theater and are deciding which movie to see, the inner minions arise. One minion wants to see the latest superhero movie, pointing out that it has been patiently waiting for the film's release for three freakin' years. Another minion steps forward, points out that it's opening week, the theater is going to be packed, and it really doesn't feel like being squashed amongst all those chatty people-besides, there is a really good comedy out that you have wanted to see as well, most likely with an almost empty theater audience. Then the wrestling match ensues. These comical minions duke it out (although it's often not so comical while the bout is occurring in our minds), pulling no punches, using everything and the kitchen sink until a victor emerges and a decision has been made.

In this simple scenario there are just two minions, but in reality, there could be many more that emerge, and the same goes for the multiple simultaneous realities that we are working with. There are hundreds, nay, thousands of minions that exist in your 'mind'; they are what help you function in the world - and that "you" I just mentioned is the first real "you" that this section discusses. All the minions collectively, you will come to realize, really answer to the first level of You. And once you start to realize it, that underlined you who is doing the realizing is the second 'you.' And, since this manual is merely a beginner's guide and all, that is where the really deep explanations are going to pause for now. But, to briefly touch on the topic so as to not fully incite outcry, let's just say that the third 'you' could be considered somewhat god-adjacent, and would probably be witnessed during the now moments in which one could potentially say that they feel "enlightened."

Evolution of the Minions

Once you have your conscious awakening you begin to employ some tools, such as meditation, to practice spending more time in the second version of you, the observer. As this "you" begins to spend more and more time being present and aware, the minions begin to lose their grip, and they take notice. These are the ego battles and things that "pull us off the path," so to speak, but really they are just moments that will become future enlightenments. But it is of utmost importance to realize and recognize that the minions will always be there. They, like you, will simply evolve.

During one of my more accelerated periods of spiritual growth, I was simultaneously studying and practicing massage and bodywork. As I grew more practiced and began to intertwine massage and bodywork with my spirituality, I created a healer minion-or rather the previous healer minion that had focused on psychology and healing my mind to its current state evolved into a healer that combines all of that knowledge, understanding, and experience to allow me to be able to provide the person with whom I am working whatever they may need at a particular moment. When I need to be the minion that likes to relax and watch basketball, the healer me steps back, aware and ready to be summoned when needed.

To start to tie this in with the previous concepts in this book, you could look at it from the perspective that there is a minion in you that is tasked with anger, like the anger discussed in section 2. Being a human and living in a dualistic reality, the fact of the matter is that there will always exist an "anger minion" inside of you. And for good reason: sometimes, anger is exactly the emotion or tool that life and enlightenment require. What's more important is your ability to harness it from the awareness of the second you, and consciously direct that energy towards future manifestations.

And this is where you really get to the juicy stuff; the stuff everyone wants to know more about: What comes after enlightenment? How did the masters of old perform their famed miracles? What exactly was meant when they said that reality is an illusion, or, to put it in slightly more modern terms, that reality is a matrix, similar to that in the movie of the same name? We'll get to that, but let's close out this little bit first.

Mastery Through Passion

Through moments of growth, awareness, perspective, and enlightenment, you will begin to see the things that make you the unique being that is you, and the joy the experience of simply being that can bring. This is when you tie in such questions such as, "What job do I want?" or "What should I do with my life?" In my case this has evolved into a dual concept of healer and teacher. For others it's artist, mathematician, or video game developer. Some people really just want to be a villager and enjoy relaxation. Others strive to develop cures for diseases. Others want to bring about the next big technological development. It matters not the lens through which your passion is focused; what matters is having an aware evolution of that passion. It is not the Mastery of that thing that is the goal, but rather the mastery and understanding of mastery itself.

This leads us to the answer to the "why" of meditation (and all that jazz). Why do we meditate? Why do we learn to control the mind? What do we do with that inner peace, that inner stillness, that quiet place? When spiritual teachers speak about non-thought, an added perspective might be to use the phrase "non-human thought." That you that exists at the second level is, indeed, observing, but it also has its own unique form of thought, which can be described as the "X marks the spot" on the treasure map of life.

To relate it to a bigger topic, let's use manifestation. You can go through this or that ritual or whichever steps, but if any part of you is creating that manifestation, at any point either during or after that initial energy wave has been emitted, is actually being run by one of the minions, then the act of manifestation is at least partly sabotaged. Crafting these grander ideas with precision to create the desired outcome requires doing so from the thinking that only the second <u>you</u> is capable of doing, and that is not achieved through "human thinking." And yet again we have encountered a topic that requires much more devotion than this beginner guide can provide, but if you continue to follow the thread, you will find the tapestry.

Now let's wrap this all up with a nice little bow. As you go through life, discovering the things that you are passionate about, examining experiences more closely, and playing the game of enlightenment, you will come to master your 'thing' while learning to operate from this mysterious second <u>you</u> that is higher consciousness. While you follow your passion and go about "normal" life, becoming increasingly skilled that which is your passion, the second <u>you</u> is learning the art of mastery. And just like in the movie *The Matrix*, that mastery becomes a "program," or software if you will. Then, when you want to learn something new, instead of going through all the same "human thinking" steps as you did before, you will be able to insert that program (understanding of mastery), and pick up that new thing much more quickly and efficiently. This is the application of science, spirituality, and meditation.

Exercises for Chapter 9

1. Hopefully, by now you've reviewed some of your earlier interests and natural passions through the exercises up to this point. Now that you have practiced examining different times in your life from a micro, up-close perspective, take a couple steps back if you will and take a more macro approach. Look for the things you do merely for the sake of being yourself, the things toward which you are naturally inclined. In my case, I always seemed to want to teach and help people heal. A close friend of mine

realized that he was always a 'protector,' a life path that took him into the armed forces and serving his country as part of his enlightenment journey. Remember that your passion can be absolutely anything: from writing and performing music to going fishing and camping every chance you get. Look for the passions and find the similarities. You will begin to see your path to mastery.

2. Begin writing down the things you feel most passionate about, as well as ways you could potentially start to focus on those things more in your life. Again, it's not about what you do; it's about being aware of what you do. Simply having these thoughts and ideas within your awareness will begin to have an effect on your reality.

Chapter 10

Those Who Can't, Teach...

Those Who Can, Do; Those Who Can't, Teach.

I've reflected on this common saying numerous times during my lifetime, and I am convinced that most have the real meaning behind this statement incorrect. Rather than implying a less-than-"professional" ability at some task as many interpret the old saying, I instead see it as describing teaching as the place to which a person comes when they have learned all they can from outside sources. At some point one realizes that everywhere they seek new information about their topic of interest, they begin to hear the same old things. When this happens, the only thing left to do to satisfy the thirst for knowledge while beginning to teach what one knows.

That is when the real schooling beings, as anyone who has ever taught will confirm. As we acquire knowledge and work towards a level of mastery, we do so from our own, unique perspective. The problem, however, is that eventually we will run out of questions to ask, and we hit a plateau. But as a quote that I recently heard and that really resonates with me suggests, "true intelligence is the ability to see things from a different perspective." And this is where teaching comes in.

As a teacher, whether in front of one student or an auditorium full of listeners, there seems to be one inevitability once you have given your spiel and proven your knowledge: questions. As it turns out, a good Q & A is the moment that all truth seekers truly relish, because, if you are lucky enough to have said the right things to the right people, you will prompt a question that even you had never considered. The years you have spent mastering your thing, whatever it may be, has put you in the place where you might not yet have all the answers, but that is only due to a lack of knowing the questions to ask. As you will discover upon being given a question, mastery itself has taught you how to easily find the answers.

Teaching, The Inevitability of Mastery

Progressing from last chapter's discussion of harnessing the power of that which you love in order to discover your passion and your route to mastery, you will eventually run into the situation I opened with. At some point, you have no teacher or knowledge source to turn to in order to further your mastery, so a new perspective must be reached. Thankfully, though, you will also experience the magic of the universe and manifestation.

One day you will be talking with someone about your passion, and they will ask you just the right question that will send you on a new train of thought. But the magic doesn't end there. As if that isn't amazing enough, the reason they will ask you that question will be because you will have ignited a spark in them, perhaps helping them discover a passion of their own, leaving them wanting to know everything that you know about the subject. Naturally, they will approach it from their perspective, which is completely unique to them and different from your own, as they begin their path to mastery. And the beginning of their journey simultaneously marks the continuation of your journey to mastery.

To get even more macro about it and add further perspective, both you and the person asking you the question have been on this path to mastery from birth (and perhaps even before), and that moment, that spark that gave you both new insight and enlightenment, was your joint manifestation on both paths of mastery. When the student is ready, the teacher will appear. Which one exactly was the student?

Egos and Minions

One thing I am fond of telling people is that we are all our own universes, or, more accurately, we each are the center of our own universe, merely bumping into other universes, which are more commonly known as other people. When you get on the topic of "spiritual knowledge" the ego can get very tricky. To help smooth the understanding, first consider this common experience for psychotherapists.

It's rather common that during a psychotherapy session a therapist will share a thought or different perspective with a client. After a period of time, the client excitedly returns to their therapist, exclaiming that they have had a breakthrough. Once they proceed to disclose their big revelation, it turns out to be the very same thing the therapist mentioned however long ago, but for the client, that realization is all theirs, and the therapist bites their tongue.

But who really lays claim to the realization? The therapist who initially posed it to the client or the client who eventually worked to understand and integrate it into their unique perspective? If you side with the therapist, you would then have to inquire about the source of the therapist's own understanding. Did their suggestion arise organically and wholly from within themselves, or did some teacher along their path utter those words to them, just as they did to their client, perhaps even having forgotten themselves that moment of knowledge acquisition because, as their client, it was a piece of enlightenment that they had to let settle into their being before "discovering"?

Oh the blessed ego, head minion in charge! Yet, the simple fact of the matter is that every person's understanding of every truth comes through their own means, from their own perspective, which, in turn, has been shaped by every 'now' moment since they had their first stirrings of consciousness. Each new understanding represents a moment on your enlightenment path and piece of your puzzle. Each understanding is uniquely yours and belongs to no one else. You are creating me to help you understand your enlightenment, and likewise, I am doing the same.

When it comes to the matters discussed in this book, this same ego battle must be attended to within the student-teacher relationship. I once joked with a spiritual teacher of mine that if the people that were paying me to coach them knew how much I learned from our conversations, they would demand payment from me. And I have a feeling that all teachers can relate to that experience. When we think about the fact that people have been exploring these concepts and discovering these truths for unknown thousands of years it really brings home the question of who really "owns" this information anyway? The possession of knowledge has been hoarded and subsequently lost throughout time. Secret societies formed around understandings of how to use the nature of truth to change reality. Wars are fought in the name of religions built upon their own systems of knowledge. The drive for more knowledge still persists, and, indeed, knowledge comes to those who are able to look for it in the right places. However, one does not pass the test by discovering this sacred yet simple knowledge;

the true test is acquiring this knowledge while at the same time dealing with the human ego.

Appreciation

As a teacher one of the best tools that you can wield is appreciation: appreciation for your own journey, but more importantly, appreciation for the journey of others, especially your students. I've seen many teachers, and myself have felt pangs of envy when a student reached a deep level of understanding in minutes of something that took me years of contemplation to grasp. But remember, like attracts like, and you get what you give. The reason that this particular knowledge has persisted over time is because it is a living, organic knowledge woven into the very fabric of this dimension, this universe, and this duality. Providing another being with the words that allows them to reach a level of enlightenment before your eyes, and being able to appreciate their process, allows you to further appreciate your own level of understanding and enlightenment, and, in turn, your refined capacity for appreciation beckons the Source to reveal more knowledge to you.

The way that this understanding arose for me was by reflecting on the psychological concept that the things you see in others, such as the things that they do that make you angry, might actually be a part of yourself that you are unaware of or in denial about, and the source of the anger is actually the denial of accepting that part of yourself. When I was able to have enough awareness and someone was 'making me angry,' I would ask which part of me was angry, and which part of me was actually similar to that person; the thought experiment evolved from there.

Although I use anger as the example here, the same process of inner examination can be used for all feelings and emotions that you initially perceive as being expressed by, emanating from, or felt for others. This gets into the concept of empathy. Empathy helps us gather additional perspectives that we can assimilate into our own spiritual development and path of enlightenment.

After a period of time observing others and being aware of how practicing empathy affected my own inner-verse, and identifying where my reactions to them were stemming from, eventually led to a level of inner peace. In turn, my experience of inner peace evolved into an appreciation for the journey of others. We are all exactly where we are supposed to be at this moment in time, perfect in our uniqueness and current experiential perspective for the source. And *that* is the meaning of life.

So teachers, appreciate your students and their journeys. When they reach a realization that you long ago understood, remember what it felt like when you experienced that mind blowing moment; from your vantage point and additional perspective, you also know how much more lies ahead for your students, and you may be reminded of all the future realizations yet to be discovered on their path. In so doing, your appreciation follows the universal law: so, too, will you instantly be reminded of all the realizations that still lay ahead of you, and the future 'you' reflects back on this shared moment of enlightenment with the present 'you.'

The lotus flower that is enlightenment is ever unfolding, limited only by the dimensions to which we open ourselves. The way to open yourself to new dimensions is through the exploration of different perspectives. What better way to access those perspectives than by teaching? Through the act of teaching you evoke a specific thread of thought from your current place of understanding; regardless of the level of understanding held by the student you are teaching, consciousness will find some way to poke through and speak to and through you, for your intent is onward and upward. Appreciating that reality and responding to the profound truths sprouted from seemingly novice students ignorant of the true meaning of their own words is a delight for the teacher, a reward for "paying the piper," and doing the so-called leg work of discovering the truths that are now able to be shared.

Teacher Qualification

Another truth about teaching that is also applicable to areas of life that include parenting and performance is that, despite your best efforts, the more you think about and prepare for it, the more you realize you can never be completely "ready." There simply is an infinite number of things to learn and attempt to perfect. So, like all things in life, you eventually will simply have to take that first step to get out there and just do it. Of course, this does not negate the fact that care and preparation should be taken before so doing. Which leads us to consider the vigor of youth and the wisdom of age.

Regardless of age, when you are young on your spiritual path, you explore many things and are an eager, adventurous student. As you progress, you have your scrapes, bumps, and bruises mixed in with grand adventures and deep rabbit holes of philosophical understanding. Through this process you begin to become more refined, confident in the truths you are now accepting. The real test of that confidence comes when you try and teach that understanding to another conscious being. Your understandings will be challenged, your beliefs will be tested, and you will either stand vigilant and proud or retreat from the dominance of a more experienced debater. This is you moving into the teacher you will become, and when that process starts is up to you. Returning to awareness of what is being done, I would only present a few things to consider.

Like the knowledge you have received from the various teachers in your life, your words, actions, and deeds will have an effect on the lives of others. Claiming to know more than you do, passing off information as truth when you know otherwise, or taking action while your ego refuses to allow you to admit that you do not know something can have an extremely negative effect on your life and the lives of the people your words and actions impact. So take care, because we do still live in a duality; what you put out comes back to you tenfold.

While I remain steadfast in my belief that your truest spiritual teacher, guide, or guru is found within and is your highest form, having proxies or physical placeholders outside yourself from whom you can seek guidance is just as important as finding students to whom you can pass on your organic knowledge. Every part of us needs a break sometimes, and that includes the teacher you, or your teacher minion; the best way for a teacher to get a vacation is to become a student again and let someone else do the teaching for a while.

When the student is ready, the teacher will appear.

Other People's Enlightenment

To bring this chapter to a close, I want to retouch upon a topic I briefly mentioned earlier but from a larger perspective. In some aspect, when you are trying to describe your enlightenment to someone, you are the teacher and they are the student. Always keep in mind that this is also true and exactly the same for them. At some point, they will reach their own level of enlightenment, and when they venture into the scary territory of trying to explain that to you, do not fall into the ego trap of forcing your enlightenment upon them. The process and words that worked for you did just that:

they worked for *you*, and what will work for them will work for *them*. So instead, I invite you to try and understand their enlightenment from *their* perspective. Who knows, it just might add to your own enlightenment.

Exercises for Chapter 10

Just the word "teacher" can conjure intense emotions from all ends of the spectrum. But think about your daily life for a minute. We all love to share the knowledge we have and what we think is right. We do this all the time; we just don't consider it teaching. Whether it comes in the form of a philosophical discussion with a friend or off-topic research with like-minded co-workers on company time, we love to talk about what we know. And if you think about it, that *is* an act of teaching. When we are sharing from our own book of life, and not some textbook of scientific knowledge, we may not realize that teaching is precisely what is happening.

1. From this new *perspective*, begin to explore the things that you really like to teach to others. While you might find that your preferred teaching topics have a lot to do with the things you discovered that you are passionate about while completing the exercises from the previous chapter, they might not be. Either way, make a list or mental note: what do you and/or would you like to teach?

2. Go out and find someone to teach that thing to, either again, or for the first time. Even if you try and fail completely, I promise you that you will find your piece of enlightenment in that experience - even if only in hindsight. Acknowledge what your higher self has always been hinting towards, and you will begin to see

real magic enter your reality. If nothing else, at
the very least you will be amazed by what your
"student" will actually teach you.

Chapter 11

What Comes After

Enlightenment?

Hopefully by this point, the title of this chapter and the idea of claiming your enlightenment does not seem quite as arrogant as it once did. The real problem rests in the collective (or not so collective) definition of the word enlightenment. To jump back to old school teachings, I will recount a well-known parable.

One day, an eager young student ran up to an enlightened master who was carrying a heavy sack down a hillside. "Master! Master! What does it mean to be enlightened?" The old master looked at the inquisitive young student, and without saying a word, set the heavy bag down by his side, stretched a little, stood up straight, and smiled. "I see," the student said. "What comes after enlightenment?" And just as before, without saying one word, the master picked the heavy sack back up, and started walking back down the hill, and at that instant the student was enlightened.

By now you may be looking at that last statement a little differently than before reading this manual. "And at that instant the student was enlightened." Was the student instantly transformed into an enlightened being that levitated around for the rest of his life? Or, did that moment provide him deeper insight into the nature of life, consciousness, and the nature of this duality that we find ourselves in? If nothing else, for the student that moment stands as one of the many brushstrokes adding to a unique soul's overall picture of enlightenment.

Life Goes On; The Only Constant is Change

As you progress down this path, you will continue to gain new perspectives, experience more flashes of enlightenment, and gain a bigger view of your unique picture of enlightenment, as well as the macro manifestation that is your life. And just like the master picking the sack back up and walking back down the hill, life continues to move forward. But the you operating in those new now moments is a changed you, a more enlightened you. Even when you are operating more on the first level, allowing the minions to be in charge, yours are now more evolved, enlightened minions.

Over the evolution of this process, moments of enlightenment will continue to appear in your life, and will astound and amaze you. The reality of duality is that there will still be "ups and downs" that occur in life, but your perspective during those times will be different. That is the true definition of enlightenment: progress, not perfection.

The most noticeable shift will be the amount of time that it takes for you to discover the meaning behind (your piece of enlightenment gained from) the events and things that happen in your life. As a result, your lived experience becomes more peaceful, and you appear to others to be wiser and "enlightened."

Duality and Humanity, Revisited

Let's return to the topic of the meaning of life: experience itself. Yet, the question remains: Exactly which experience or perspective is the right one? Sure, we strive to become "enlightened," and devote part of our lives to a "spiritual path," perhaps even becoming one with everything and feeling the presence of God in everyone...or whatever. But if God wanted to just experience God, then why are *we* here? We are here to experience a uniquely human life, with various degrees of "god awareness." In the end, isn't every path and every experience is an opportunity to experience the concept of god?

They are moments like these, moments you are deep in meditative thought, in which you will sometimes find yourself thinking in circles. And this is also the time when humanity is just bursting with fun things to do, minions to create and evolve, and new perspectives on life to be gained from the level one 'you' place. The world/reality/illusion/matrix can be a wonderful and fascinating place once you start exploring the different perspectives (dimensions) that are out there. (Easter Egg: Was that a new definition of dimensions that I just saw?) You are both the designer and participant in a veritable amusement park of our own design, your own virtual reality or real life sim world, and you can learn how to operate in it more effectively.

Perspectives and common sayings from teachers of old have been sprinkled throughout this manual, but keep in mind that there are many left unsaid that you are already aware of, and which are out there for you to discover. Which brings us back to the topic of karma, or the universal law of attraction that reminds us that you get back what you put out.

One quote I want to return to, first and foremost, is: "It's not about what you do, it's about being aware of what you do." You may choose to test limits, push boundaries, and see just what you are capable of, but do so from a place of awareness. Realize that in a duality, which is the general operating law of this dimension in which your physical being or vessel is rooted; every action spurs a reaction, and there is an exchange of energy that takes place.

This is where I propose yet another new perspective on an old thought: Duality versus Non-dualism, or the middle path. Earlier in my development, after I had devoted myself to meditation for a few years, I had come to find an overall state of peace, that was, quite possibly the fabled inner peace that has been spoken about for eons. And not too long after that, I got bored. Peace can be nice, but at certain points in our lives, a little un-peace is what we really, deep down, enjoy. Evidence of this can be seen throughout history, when immense periods of change followed turmoil, which, in turn, was often the result of stagnation.

For me, that peace was the starting point for further exploration. One of my early inner goals came around the age of thirteen or fourteen, when I was impacted by the death of my father. He died of a heart attack, and although there is a long history behind that, the long and short of it is that at the time I realized that heart problems may be in my genetics, so I should start working on easing my burdens as soon as possible. Being young and rather innocent at the time, I pinpointed stress as the biggest area of concern, and began my quest to master stress management, eventually achieving a certain level of mastery by finding inner peace. This is that's not to say that I am the most peaceful person on the planet, or even peaceful half the time these days, but, in moments of crisis in which peace is needed, that particular evolved minion is on call and standing by.

I hypothesize that I became bored with peace because I no longer had a place to focus the practice of mastery. Thus, from that place of boredom, I turned my focus toward the exploration of duality to gain further perspective. As evidenced in my life by my struggles with alcohol at that time, I experienced life as a set of highs and lows, ups and downs. A decade later, I find myself pondering the middle path of non-dualism. To tie this thought in with section 2 of this manual, let's return to the topic of acceptance. Perhaps non-dualism or the middle path is not the denial or non-seeing/non-acknowledgement of duality, but rather the full awareness and acceptance of duality, the yin and the yang, the dark and the light, in order to better operate in this current now moment of your life.

Harness duality to create reality.

The Return to Stillness, Meditation, and You

What comes after Enlightenment? Life, awareness, further meditations, and new moments of enlightenment. The minions that have been with you on this journey so far have succumbed to your understanding that they are not in control, and instead you have a really good working relationship. Every once in a while, a new one may emerge or an old one may get out of hand, but this is now a cause for delight. After all, each challenge now allows you to experience a new moment of enlightenment right?

If I had one piece of advice for all who are on the path, the number one tool and true manual for the soul is the practice of meditation. The still focused attention on the present moment. For that is where all the instructions that you will ever need can be found. The reality of duality is that you will have immense highs, and at some point your rock bottom low; you will experience periods of immense spiritual growth and the feeling of being one with everything, as well as times when you doubt your explorations into these thoughts, along with your sanity and the conclusions you have reached. No matter the moment, no matter what is going on, in an instant, a mere millisecond, you can go into meditation, find that place of inner stillness, non-human thought, communion with your higher self, and regain your connection. Knowing this, and being aware enough to use this tool when needed, just might be its own form of enlightenment.

Enlightenment, Magic, and the True Power of Now

To begin to wrap it up, let's briefly work this theory through to its culmination. You've worked on this process of reviewing moments in your life that beg reviewing, developing, and evolving, while adopting a more 'enlightened' view of life along the way. At some point, you will have reviewed all that needs reviewing, and you will be fully present in that Now moment, with no distractions of past 'unsolved mysteries.'

In that place, in that Now moment, with all your minions quietly awaiting your instructions for future manifestations and perceptions of reality, what exactly does come next? What is the next thing that you will see? Better yet, what if you and a hundred friends were to join together, in that same place, in that Now moment? What would you collectively see in the *next* Now moment? What do we *all* collectively choose to see in our next Now moment from the vantage point of the current Now moment?

Those are a few of the questions that will lead to the rediscovery of true "magic" in the world. All it takes is a little (mass) awareness. But hey, one step, or soul, at a time.

Future Dimensions of Thought

To add one more thought and perspective for you to chew on to prepare for future manuals requires a return to the story at the beginning of this chapter. Recall the bit about when the old master picked the sack back up and started walking back down the hill, and that in that instant the student became enlightened. Exactly when did the "instant of enlightenment" occur? As Einstein said, "Time only exists so that everything isn't happening at once." Combining that with the perspective posed in this manual, when it says, "in that instant the student was enlightened," that instant could happen decades later, in a moment of reflection during meditation.

And this brings us full circle back to the journal entry I wrote after that blackout inspired my first meditation. Our moments of intuition and insight could be messages from our future enlightened self, sending us back the information so that we progress faster. Or perhaps, since that is still a future version of us only separated by time, the reason that you experience that intuition or significance (like that feeling of significance I had as a young boy looking out the car window, contemplating if I was on a TV show) is the result of that future you reflecting on that moment and seeing the enlightenment in it. That feeling of intuition is potentially a form of feeling the reverberations of enlightenment through time.

So what exactly is time? Deeper understandings start to reveal the not-so-fixed nature of time. We currently perceive time through a collective consciousness, and that experience of time is really more of a dimension of thought than anything else. And when needed, we can choose to set it aside to further explore the true nature of the universe and what may lie beyond. As so, time is a choice, one made by the Source so that you can experience this now moment and find the enlightenment held within it. Now, doesn't that kind of give you a different perspective to consider when you start to feel insignificant while pondering matters such as God, The Universe, and the billions of stars and galaxies that comprise just the physical dimension/universe that we *can* "see"?

A Beginner's Manual indeed.

Have fun exploring, and remember: it's not about what you do, it's just about being aware of what you do.

Exercise for Chapter 11

In whatever place you currently find yourself on this journey, it is still right Now, and what you will see next is your choice. If nothing else, take this concept, and begin to see and connect the dots to gain a picture of your own enlightenment. But that's not all. From this Now moment moving forward, evolve the theory. Instead of merely connecting the dots, choose to paint by numbers from this point on. Let's begin to co-create the reality that we, the real us, truly want to see.

Closing

When I began writing this manual, I had a grand idea of an all-encompassing guide to everything that is life and enlightenment. It didn't take long for me to realize how difficult a task that is, if not impossible. Not to mention the number of pages it would take to explain all of that. Who would read it? It was at that point that I went back to the working title and changed it to *Manual for the Soul: A Beginners Guide*. And from the perspective put forth in this manual, perhaps keeping the mindset of a beginner is really the secret all along. A full cup holds no more liquid after all.

That being said, there are still many topics to cover and perspectives to explore. And so, this Manual for the Soul is actually the first part in a series of manuals exploring all that there is to discover. An Operator's Guidebook to the Universe, if you will. You are the Operator in this body, experiencing the amusement park that is reality right?

Some upcoming manuals include Manual for the Mind, and Manual for the Body, with many more to follow. It's time to take part in the conscious evolution of humanity; physically, mentally; emotionally, spiritually, and energetically, to help create the future that we all know is possible. It's time to evolve forward or break free from the dogmas, traditions, and separation of the old, and move into the world of a connected humanity.

To find out more, as well as read helpful blogs and other information pertaining to your personal development, you can visit http://tribeingmbe.com and access further content. The contact e-mail for Tri-Being: Mind. Body. Energy. is contact@tribeingmbe.com

As a tool to help you through this process, I have developed a workbook that can be used in conjunction with this manual. It is free gift for people who have purchased this manual as a way to say thank you. It can be accessed on my webpage at tribeingmbe.com/MFTS. The password to enter is **Aware**.

Whatever your age, background, religious/spiritual beliefs or current place in life, your own unique form of Enlightenment is developing within you. If you need to, find someone such as myself or another person you feel qualified enough to provide you with a new perspective that will help you further your growth. And remember,

It's not about what you do; it's just about being AWARE of what you do.

About The Author

Jordan Finneseth often refers to himself as a meandering mystic and student of the world. Like many in his Millennial generation, he pursued higher education directly after high school, obtaining a bachelors and master's degree in clinical/counseling psychology. During that time, he also began meditating and developing himself spiritually, releasing ties to any specific dogma to instead discover their commonalities.

After working as a therapist for a few years, Jordan directed his interest towards healing the body and obtained an associate's degree in Medical Massage. Since that time he has studied various healing traditions - physical, mental, and energetic - to become an all-around healer and Spiritual Development Coach.

Manual for the Soul: A Beginner's Guide is Jordan's introductory book of what will become a series of Manuals taking ancient, complex ideas and bringing them forward into this new millennium. His goal is simple: To give people back their spiritual power which has been veiled from their sight for too long. Collectively we hold the power to change the world, and it starts with the Awareness of this fact.

Tri-Being: Mind. Body. Energy.

It's time to realize all that we are.